Sweetgum Slough

Sweetgum Slough

✦

A 1930's Florida Memoir

Stories of Joy

and Hookworms

and Red-tailed Fishes

Claire Karssiens

iUniverse, Inc.

New York Bloomington

Sweetgum Slough
A Florida Memoir

iUniverse books may be ordered through booksellers or by contacting:

iUniverse
1663 Liberty Drive
Bloomington, IN 47403
www.iuniverse.com
1-800-Authors (1-800-288-4677)

ISBN: 978-1-935-27870-2 (pbk)
ISBN: 978-1-935-27873-3 (ebk)

Library of Congress Control Number: 2009931104

Printed in the United States of America

iUniverse rev. date: 06/30/2009

To the precious memory of six years in the Florida backwoods with my family: to my father, who could find humor in anything, even the disease that took his young life; to my mother, who believed that everything was possible and proved it; to my lovely and talented sister, who taught me to look for beauty in unexpected places; and to my brother, our scholar and sportsman, our war hero who died too young.

I miss them.

Acknowledgments

I want to thank the North Georgia Mountain writers: Ted Slaughterbach, our talented teacher and, especially, Ann Mather and Fritzie Seifert who gave me so much help for so long. The Sarasota writers offered great critiques and good advice. Special thanks to Edee Fiore and Rena Bloxham and to Janet Kaplan for her encouragement. B.J. Julian prepared my manuscript with love and skill and to her I am most grateful. Terry Tarsnane cheered me on all the way from the Netherlands. Most of all, I thank my husband, Janpiet, whose help, support, and patience made it possible for me to write this book.

Contents

My Father's Child

by Claire Karssiens

There was a time
when all things were
as they should have been.
A shining-pine-needle time
when shallow rain ditches
spread joy and hookworms
and red-tailed fishes.
And I was my father's child.

When razorback rooters
watched from the palmettos
and the shadow of buzzards
soothed over the land,
and salmon-gut guavas gave
their scent from the hedges.
And I was my father's child.

When a soft fall of rain
moved silently on
in front of the saplings
in the distance and gone.
And all things were
as they should have been
when I was my father's child.

Baby Ray

Belle Boggs knew and told me all about it as we were sitting in the privy eating guavas. The girls' privy was an intriguing place, especially when I could manage to get out there at the same time as Belle. It wasn't easy, but it could happen on days when the teacher looked distracted or when Mr. Whatley came to see her, and the enamored pair sat on the front porch speaking in soft, secret voices together.

First, we would slip around behind the outhouse where the guava bushes grew verdantly, nurtured by the friendly privy. Then, like two young monkeys, we would pick a couple of big, yellow guavas and bite into them at once, exposing their lusty pink interiors, seeds imbedded in perfect patterns in their fragrant flesh. Moments later, sitting on the smooth holes in the little, dark vertical room, our six-year-old legs dangling inches from the wooden floor, I would be almost overcome by the euphoria of stolen freedom, the taste and scent of the guava so close to my face, and the rich odor rising from the mysterious dank mass—made ever more pungent by the rhythmic kneading of maggots just several feet below my bare, white bottom.

And added to all that, there was the excitement of Belle beside me, gnawing her guava and enriching me with tales of love and sex as they were expressed in her own household and throughout the little rural community of Sweetgum Slough. She spared no one, and she knew how to entertain. Her imagination crackled like a sparkler once she got herself ignited. Sitting in the dim light of the privy with our cotton underpants hanging around our ankles, kicking our heels against the lower support of the privy seat, I could just see the smoky features of Belle's dark face, her tadpole irises slipping across the whites of her eyes and the growth of strangely light, unwashed, and tangled curls like a large, messy collection of dusty wood shavings dumped on her head. We were so caught up in our little privy world we would whoop with laughter and squeal with delight until some other child, waiting to replace us in the privy, told the teacher on us.

Belle came from a big, rowdy family of adults who lived in a shack up the hardroad. They were all dark-skinned people, and some of them had nappy hair. It was whispered about that they had Negro blood. In the early 1930s, the South, much less small white rural hamlets in Florida, had not begun to recover from its racial stupor. So if such were the case, it was something to hide, but no one in Sweetgum Slough had either the courage or the lack of sense to question any of the Boggs family. Belle's older brothers, like Bird Dog, who was handsome and strong and inseparable from his guns and his horse, were wild and dangerous and went on shooting sprees around their yard for fun.

I don't know what they did to earn a living. That didn't interest me. I think it didn't interest them either. They were there, and they were colorful and noisy. Children liked and admired Belle's brothers, but the community avoided them until Bird Dog married Eulice McCracken, who was just fourteen. That union drew the Boggs into things a bit more, and for a while and out of curiosity, one or two of them appeared in the little Sweetgum church on Sunday. Everyone was sad when Bird Dog was killed by his own horse.

In those days, I had a father and a mother, a brother and a sister. Nothing important was missing. Most people were poor in 1932, but my father and grandfather managed to salvage enough from their losses in real estate in Tampa to survive the stock market crash. My father bought two large tracts of virgin land in the piney woods of central Florida. He was a laughing, creative man who viewed his financial disaster as a good reason to take his young family into an adventure that would live with all of us for the rest of our lives.

He had a strong, new house built for us that smelled of fresh pine all over. And we had a mule named Sparkplug, a black car, a black Great Dane named Balder, and a black man called Enzo Hendry who came and walked behind Sparkplug, plowing our new fields where my father's fledgling orange trees would later struggle against torrential rain or a winter freeze or orangedogs— beautiful and lethal caterpillars that we plucked from the tender young trees and, with clenched jaws, ground under our feet.

I had a teacher, too. Her name was Beulah Cockshot, and she was fat and hard-faced. She pinned her dyed black hair down with big bobby clips to affect waves around her broad, powdered face. Sometimes stiff strands escaped the clips, giving her a misleading, abandoned look. She was probably about fifty, but she seemed old to me. She drove a Model T Ford with a rumble seat. It was a tiny, funny car, and she liked to park it under a tree in the churchyard across the hardroad from the school. When she left in the afternoon, she had to crank her little car, and she did that expertly with her big, strong arms. I was afraid of her.

The school was a small, white, wooden building trimmed in green. Part of its shingled roof stood under a great oak tree that shaded the open porch on hot spring and summer days when dirt daubers sang their nasal song and built little earthen igloos along the eaves of the porch. I liked the porch. From there, if I got to school before the other children, I could sometimes see a mother screech owl and her tiny young ones lined up beside her on a limb like little furry kittens. And when my friends arrived, I liked to sit on the porch with them or play Kitty Wants a Corner with Lutie Bea, Belle, Nina and Dorcus Tatum, Arla, and Wilene.

Playing that game with Dorcus carried high risk and added to the excitement. Dorcus was big, sullen, and dumb. When she didn't end up with one of the four posts during the scramble, she would give me a slap across my face, sling me down the steps, and take my post.

Inside, there was one large room with an elevated stage at the far end and four windows in each of the side walls. In winter, the glass windows could be pulled closed. In the fall and spring, when the Florida heat brought all of life to a standstill by midday, the windows were open, propped up by pieces of firewood. And there was a kind of crisscross wire screen, with diamond-shaped apertures large enough to permit a small bird to fly through and hunt for spiders. I think the wire was there to keep us from climbing in and out. We climbed everything that stood still long enough for us to get a foothold.

A large wood-burning stove in the center of the room kept us warm on cold days. Mrs. Cockshot and some of the big eighth-grade boys would build a fire in the stove, and we would all stand around it and warm our hands and then turn around and warm our tails. Sometimes we burned ourselves on the stove. Nobody cried about that except me.

When the weather was cold, most of the children had coughs and sniffles. Nina Tatum wore two perfect patches of yellow custard in her nostrils all winter. She managed to keep them right in place like two airtight stoppers, and she had to breathe through her mouth. She was one of my best friends. Nina was sweet and quiet and generous like all the Tatums, except Dorcus.

It was dark in the schoolroom, even on bright sunny days, because of the shadow cast by the big oak tree outside and the dark green paint on the walls. I never asked if that color was a choice, and I suspect the paint was issued to the school by the county or one of the many New Deal agencies. Sometimes it was almost impossible to see Raphael's Madonna of the Chair, which hung in a round frame without glass on the wall near the front door. Close to the front door stood a bookcase full of old textbooks, and Mrs. Cockshot needed a flashlight to find books in that corner. In fact, unless one was lucky enough to be seated near the windows, it was hard to see anything. There was no electricity or any other form of lighting, except when we had the Christmas program at night. Then kerosene lamps were provided by people in the community.

Mrs. Cockshot kept her desk up on the stage most of the time. After she built the fire, she would go up there to her desk and look through her books, licking her thumbs and fingers to turn pages. She kept a big bell on her desk that she would ring loudly at eight o'clock to let us know it was time to go to our seats and to summon a few children who were still hanging around the shingled structure that protected the open well or in either of the two privies. Whenever Mrs. Cockshot got up from her desk, her dress caught in the crack between her big, hard buttocks, and when she turned around to write on the board or pull a map down, we could see it snuggled in there. Some of the older children were brave enough to look at each other and giggle. Most of us were too terrified to do anything, but little Cooter Crawley would laugh out loud and get a whipping when the rest of us went to recess.

Our desks were in rows and nailed to the floor. The first graders' desks were smaller than the others. There were only four or five of us in the first grade, and I was scared a lot of the time because I had to sit on the other side of the room from my big sister, who was in seventh grade. I was afraid that I would not know when to go to the recitation bench. Every time Mrs. Cockshot called a group to the bench, I wondered if I should go. And one time, I wet my pants.

After that my sister told me to look at her each time a group was called. If I should go, she would hold up her long yellow pencil. As a consequence of that agreement, I spent most of my time with my eyes fixed on my sister and her pencil. If the pencil so much as moved vertically, I would be halfway out of my seat. This in itself added to my anxiety, because Mrs. Cockshot didn't like any tomfoolery. Even when people whispered, she would rustle her switches and holler, "I never was so *sick* and *tired!*" Then we would pale and try not to look at each other, all but Belle, whose fearless gaze never wavered. Even the big boys were afraid of Mrs. Cockshot and her switches. When my sister's signal finally came, like a yellow beacon in this dark green sea, I walked breathlessly to the bench ahead of my classmates. We faced the chart and read Baby Ray.

The chart hero wore puffy Victorian romper pants and had curly, yellow hair on his large head. The chart may have been older than Mrs. Cockshot. It was so faded, everything was yellow and beige and gray except the lettering. We stared at the chart like newly hatched chickens viewing their mother for the first time. And we stared at the big black letters on the first page: "Baby

Ray." Mrs. Cockshot read the words out loud, and we read the words out loud together and individually. Then she flipped the first page over the top of the chart.

"Baby Ray has two cunning kittens," it said. And there he was again. Only this time, there were two kittens with him. One was chasing a ball of yarn, the other leaping for a butterfly. They did not look like my big black and white cat, Maxie. They didn't look like cats. But Baby Ray didn't look like a person either. I wondered what cunning kittens could be and why this strange-looking child wore bulging bloomers. Wilene, Delano, and Cooter fretted on the bench. They couldn't read the words. They didn't know they were words. Belle and I listened and learned to read.

Wilene Stitchfield was crippled and had to wear long cotton stockings, even on hot days. She carried one shriveled, useless arm close to her crooked body, and her heavy red hair, the color of strong tea, was wound around her head in a braid. I sat as far from her on the bench as I could, because she smelled of dried urine and kitchen grease. Sometimes she had fits and fell on the floor and chewed her tongue until pink foam bubbled from her mouth. Her big brother, Clegg, knew what to do, and then Mrs. Cockshot would let them go home. The solemn boy would put his arms around the pale, stunned Wilene and lead her down the hardroad to their little house about two miles away beside a pond.

The Stitchfields were mountain people, shy and illiterate. Somehow, they had wandered down to Florida from North Carolina with a handful of possessions and worked some tired fields as sharecroppers for the Dawkins, whose ancestors had claimed a lot of land and built a big, unpainted homestead surrounded by outbuildings. Plump little Ducie Stitchfield plowed their acres barefoot and wore a poke bonnet to shade her face and short, fat neck from the hot sun. Her husband, known to the neighborhood as Ole Stitch, chewed Red Mule tobacco and asked Belle or me to read his mail, which he collected from his wobbly mailbox. It stood with others like it under the oak tree in front of the school. His mail came from places like Montgomery Ward and wasn't very interesting to Belle or me, but we were happy to oblige him, and each time we read to him, he gave us a little, red, metal mule that he lifted from his tobacco cakelet with the tip of his pocket knife.

Delano Whatley was all brown and plump with baby fat. On cold days, he wore a sweater or warm shirt under his blue overalls. But his smooth, little feet were always bare. In spring and summer when hot weather came, the shirt or sweater was removed, and his brown dimpled shoulders appeared under his overall straps. His eyes were as big and brown as pine knots and decorated with calf-long eyelashes. Delano was slow to learn to read and figure, but his beauty, his gaiety, and his precocious country antics made him my best friend. We were both five years old when we started to school, but Delano could already bridle a horse and ride it lickety-split through the palmettos. He could crack a whip and climb higher in a tree than anyone.

One of his older sisters, Ruby, was in the seventh grade with my sister. The rest of the Whatleys were all grown and helping their parents farm the land and care for a herd of scrub cattle that roamed the fenceless back prairies.

An older sister lived and worked somewhere near Tampa. She was Jessie, a slim girl of about twenty. Everyone knew that she was Delano's real mother, but the circumstance of his birth was not a subject to question in Sweetgum Slough. At that time, having a child out of wedlock was a sin and a major scandal.

Delano's grandmother, Murl Whatley, came from the Dawkins clan—respected, God-fearing people. It was hard for her to hold her head high in the face of such a disgrace. But she was also a kind and courageous woman of strong character. So when the baby was born, she took him from the distressed and grateful Jessie and brought him to Sweetgum Slough. She named him Delano, and the Whatleys raised him as their own child. Mr. Whatley positioned himself more as a disengaged observer in this unlikely arrangement.

The little boy was a smiling, joyful child, loved by his big family, included in everything by all his young aunts and uncles and mothered with tender affection by Sadie, his favorite aunt who called him Bubby. And all of them protected him from the knowledge of his disgrace. But everyone knew, including Belle Boggs, who told me all about it in the privy.

After a session with Belle in the privy, even the tenth page of Baby Ray could not gain my undivided attention. I was a little wary of Belle. But she was intelligent, wise, and imaginative. I liked her wily ways. Most of all, I was fascinated by her wanton vulgarity. She had nerve, too. As soon as she learned to write, she began passing notes to me. Sometimes, right on the recitation bench, she would skillfully slide a scrap of paper to me. "Baby Ray shits in his britches."

Or she would walk by my desk on her way to the well for a drink of water and tuck a note under my book. "If you want to see me do it with Melvin tomorrow, come to school early, in the corner where the powmetters is at."

Sometimes she would send a note down a whole line of desks. "Miz Cockshot does it with ole man Whatley."

Or, "I showed Carter Mosly my booty yestiddy. JB want to see yores."

I had to be selective in the array of learning opportunities Belle offered, but she was a brilliant teacher. She helped me survive the coming six years in the Sweetgum School with strength and laughter.

Hermia and Lysander

My mother liked to hunt for things. On days when she was searching, her face was bright with purpose, her step firm. Her tilted eyes deepened green and focused. We all knew that it was within the power of each of us to challenge her just by mentioning a lost item. But in this new rural setting, richer opportunities lay waiting for her with every dawn.

A neighbor gave my mother a flock of fifteen guinea fowl to protect her from the snakes she feared. Those paranoid birds did set up an ear-ripping alarm at the sight of a snake. They did the same thing at the sight of our car as we drove down the lane. Or if they spied me running home from school, they rushed shrieking and flapping, ugly beaks open, rigid tongues protruding, skull horns erect like miniature shark fins, and disappeared into the palmettos leaving a trail of delicately spotted gray feathers behind them. At night, they roosted, like the jungle birds they were, on the upper limbs of the tall pine trees around our house. And sometimes, in the morning, we found small hard eggs on the pine needles under the trees. But that was unusual. They were furtive about their nests and preferred to hide them in the brush somewhere, laying a new egg there each day and mysteriously disappearing from the flock to incubate the clutch.

This habit provided my mother with a reliable alternative. If nothing else were lost, the illusive guinea nest could still be found. I once caught her hiding behind a tree, observing a guinea hen as it picked its way along, separate from the flock, pa-track pa-tracking in the sunshine. And I have watched my mother stepping through the huckleberry bushes, arms crossed over her bosom like the Virgin but with her eyes cast down rather than heavenward. And sometimes she would be rewarded by a nest full of warm little eggs while a hysterical guinea mother whipped her teammates into a frenzied uprising.

Guinea eggs taste like toadstools smell when you pull the fungus up from the earth: like a strong, tasty mixture of dirt and mold. Half-incubated, they are better left in the nest where they will turn into the planet's most repulsive babies, already stamped by the unmistakable personality of the guinea fowl. But my mother would become radiant at her discovery, as though she herself had squatted there in the huckleberries and produced those little hot eggs.

Other days, she would follow Enzo Hendry as he plowed our new fields behind Sparkplug, my mother's small-boned form a sharp contrast to the massive black man hunched and silent over the plow. I would see her hopping over furrows, bending to claim a dirt-encrusted prize, dusting it off, stopping now and then to examine something else in the freshly plowed earth where Indians camped long ago, or to watch a covey of quail burst into flight in front of the startled mule.

Enzo said nothing, but his big face grew ever darker and more taut than usual. My mother's presence made him uneasy. He feared that he might do or say something she would misinterpret. He knew that black men had to be silent and aloof around white women, so he tried to respond to my mother as though he weren't quite there. Even when she showed him a new treasure for her growing collection of prehistoric arrowheads and tools, he barely whispered, "Yesum" and wiped the sweat from his face with one large, polished hand. And he was afraid of the Great Dane, our family guardian, so he kept an eye on Balder, who took advantage of poor Enzo's fear, teasing the intimidated man. Pointing his bony rear upward, paws flat on the ground in front of him like the Sphinx, the big dog barked and wagged his friendly tail at the sky.

On my way to school in the morning, I could see this odd procession in the distant field: Sparkplug, Enzo Hendry, and my mother, followed by Balder. And I knew that she would stay there searching for the Holy Grail until the sun grew too hot.

Looking in the other direction, I could see my father kneeling beside one of his young trees, and with sudden excitement, I realized that he was budding—the delicate and complicated process of slipping a fine shoot into the bark of a mother tree and wrapping it with a paraffin-soaked cloth to protect it. I would then hurry along to school knowing that I could watch him when I came home in the afternoon.

I liked to watch my father when he was doing things. He was unskilled and miscast in his role of grover, but he had a passionate belief in his ability though he made grand and small mistakes and laughed and swore his way through all of them. I loved to be near him when he worked, because he was like a huge, mischievous playmate—a fellow schemer.

I delighted in his originality. He invented an array of profane expressions, which I absorbed as fast as he could produce them. And one morning when Mrs. Cockshot was putting us through her daily Bible quiz, she asked me to tell her the Savior's full name. In a strong voice, I let her know that it was Jesus Jehovsky Christ, Jr. She made no comment. Nor did her big, bland face show that the answer was either right or wrong. She was becoming more proficient in concealing the fact that I often knew things she didn't know.

On summer evenings, we children sat with our father on our front porch where he told us stories about life in an Amazon rain forest. He made the steaming, layered foliage come alive, shriek, writhe and chatter. Jungle animals were comedians and villains, and the protagonist, whatever it might be, wound its way through these tales with humor, skill and daring and usually survived. If it appeared to me that the hero may not triumph, or that he might actually be devoured or strangled by the villain anaconda or eaten by the black jaguar, I would cry and beat my father's chest with my fists until the story took a better turn. But sometimes, he would let the worst prevail no matter what I did, and I would run outraged to tell my mother and seek comfort from her.

When my rich cousins came to visit, evenings on the porch were still livelier, and everyone participated. These two boys, about the ages of my sister and brother, were my father's nephews from Tampa and unaccustomed to the sounds and scents of the rural night. The sudden scream of a bobcat or the invasive odor of a hungry skunk both frightened and thrilled them, and they would inch a little closer to my father's chair. They liked to visit us in our primitive domain, where they took moonlit shower-baths in the backyard while my brother pumped cold water over them, and they ate my mother's food that she prepared as her mother and grandmother had done before her, and which those ladies, in turn, had learned from their black servants.

My imaginative cousins always managed to stay longer than planned, and we loved the city excitement they brought with them. They knew the latest popular songs and taught them to my sister and me, and they spoke in the northern-accented voices of my father's family about Fred Astair, Ginger Rogers, and Jean Harlow. Most of all, they ruined their fine shoes, ripped their expensive clothes, and learned to go barefoot and shirtless.

My father goaded all of us into telling ghost stories at night. His own voice and eerie laughter dominated. My cat and I would take our place in his lap, and I would listen and lisp my contributions to the story for as long as I was able to speak or until it became so dark that I couldn't see their faces anymore and my cat left to catch lightening bugs. Then I would press my face against my father's chest, like lying cheek down on a sun-warmed dock, and I would listen to the liquid beat of his heart bumping at the pilings below, and the ebb tide of my slumber floated the remains of their stories out to sea with me. Later, I would awaken for a moment as he placed me in my bed, and though I couldn't see his face above me in the darkness, I knew how it would look. I knew, because it was the look he reserved for his seedlings and me.

My parents were always in love and usually with each other. Although her own mother was strict and traditional and kept to rigid religious standards like most of her southern sisters, my mother had a natural freedom of being. She was descended from the great families of South Carolina. But she was a kind of love child—sired by the Grandeur of the Old South, conceived by the wind, and born to the green and uncontaminated spirit of young Florida.

The lean figure of my father was attractive to women, and he could have accepted their attention as his just due. He flirted by instinct, like a grand blond lion. My mother's yearnings, however, were more romantic and ethereal than physical. When she fell in love with my father's handsome surgeon in Tampa, she would stand before our kitchen sink, languidly washing dishes and putting them, dripping with soap suds, into a rack while she sang current songs with titles like "My Silent Love" and lyrics that started, "I reach for you like I reach for a star, worshiping you from afar." Sometimes, a soapy dish would slip from her hand and circle around the linoleum on the kitchen floor, unnoticed. Or she would sit at her piano and play Franz Liszt's "Liebestraum" in a tempo so sagging it seemed as though she had fed those white ivory teeth a stultifying potion. As she played, leaning from side to side, her eyes closed, her perfect profile framed by the natural waves of her auburn hair with its little chignon at the nape of her neck, I could tell that she was not available to me. And I would leave the room to look for one of my pets. Or to climb a tree and wait until it passed.

My parents' superficial estrangements were as short-lived as dreams. Like children, they soon returned to each other and to their intimate, playful relationship. Again, they would be best friends and lovers on their way to the candy store in the sky, laughing, jostling, and planning for some unimaginable and unobtainable treat.

With my life in control at school, some of the hours there were close to physically painful unless I was outside playing with my friends or we were rehearsing for the Christmas program. I could see our house from my window at school, and if I saw my father drive his car through the gate with Balder's black head hanging out of the back window like a huge, handsome car gargoyle, I would cry from longing to be with them. Or if I caught a glimpse of my mother standing in our front yard with her binoculars, gazing up into the treetops, I could get into an almost uncontrollable state of needing the scent and touch of her.

   When school was finally over on such days, I ran home with all the same
excitement a child feels when she flies across the white sands and throws
herself into the sweet, warm waters of our sparkling Gulf of Mexico. I never
knew what I would find there, what lovely fragile shell waited just under the
surface, what glowing, strange little fish darted over the bottom, what giant
wave I could catch and ride all the way to everywhere. To be home with that
great child-man and his sweet, eccentric and romantic wife was the promise
the universe made to me and kept at the end of every day.

A Gift

Our arms and hands hooked over the top slats of the wooden fence, Delano and I looked down with solemn faces. Four young steers lay dead below us. Air from their lungs was still passing through the vocal apparatus in their necks, which produced a ghostly quartet of steady, monotonous drones. As I studied their great dead eyes, I thought they looked sad and disappointed.

Delano turned to me. "They always beller some. It don't mean nothin' 'cause they good and dead." Delano's word could be taken in good faith in all matters bucolic. He was wise and informed for his seven years, and I listened to him. I nodded, and we climbed down. It was butchering time at the Whatleys, and the whole day still lay unexamined ahead of us.

All week, the Whatley brothers and little Delano had been riding the back prairies, selecting choice steers from their herd, cutting them off, and rounding them up. The older boys were experts and spent their evening hours weaving handsome long leather whips, which they cracked with skill over the bony backs of their scrub cattle. They rubbed lard into their saddles to protect the leather, and they polished their fat-flanked cowponies, who had names like Buckshot and Piedy.

Delano rode barefoot and bareback, his strong little legs hooked as firmly as ice tongs into the belly of his mount, his fingers tight on the reins. Fastened there like a small woodland parasite, the boy and his horse-host galloped through the palmettos to head off a wayward heifer and leaped over fallen trees. They splashed through black ponds, uprooting lily pads. And sometimes Delano rode standing up on the back of his galloping pony.

The older boys smiled at Delano's antics. They shook their heads in mock exasperation and said things like, "Look at that little booger go," or "He ain't got a bit a sense cuttin' the fool like that," or "Little natural-born mess!" And in their home at night after a long day, when they played their guitars and banjos and sang long whining songs together, Delano always listened in the lamplight or curled up asleep on the floor at their feet.

The Whatleys and the Dawkins, Mrs. Whatley's parents, were descendents of early Anglo-Scot settlers in Florida and respected landowners. Over the years, they had built up the largest homestead and the biggest herd of scrub cattle in the county. The Whatley's weathered house was given to them by the Dawkins as a wedding present. It was an old house then, but it seemed to be rejuvenated there among ancient live oaks when the Whatleys moved in to raise their six children. There was plenty of room, and later when Jessie, to her family's dismay, brought Delano into the world, he had the run of the place. From the time he began to walk, he wandered throughout the house and in and out of the outbuildings like an amiable chicken, befriended and cared for by everyone in the family, but only his young aunt Sadie gave him her unconditional love.

The Whatleys were industrious, hardworking people, who farmed for themselves and their animals. But they were first and foremost cattle people, and that made them prosperous enough to keep a Model T Ford parked in front of the big gray house. And they gained even more respect in the community when they acquired the first Brahma bull in that part of Florida. He was expensive for those hard times in the 1930s, but the frugal Whatleys were told that he would improve the quality of their stock and soon pay his way as he sired little half-breed Brahmas with the forlorn scrub cows.

He was a monstrous white animal with his wobbly hump on his back, his long, drooping rabbit ears, and a thick neck-lap that seemed to hang from just under his dark muzzle. He rumbled deep in his throat as he walked freely throughout the unfenced countryside, his huge head nodding with each step. Sometimes he would stop, draw in a sharp breath, and produce a series of high-pitched screeches, sucking in air between each one. Then he would lower his head, roll his big black eyes back to the whites and, with his sharp hooves, hurl clumps of dirt and grass over his massive shoulders. I was filled with terror at the sight of the great, ghostly bull.

Delano laughed and said, "That ole bull sure can sing!" And he named the bull Gene Autry. The Whatleys thought that was a fine name for their bull. In fact, everyone in Sweetgum Slough liked the name, and they called him Autry for short. And sometimes he was called Ole Autry—the addition of "Ole" as an honorary title was awarded to any member of the community who distinguished himself in any way at all.

Autry lumbered and rumbled up and down the hardroad, grazed the back prairies and rested in the shade of the live oaks, chewing his cud. But he was faithful to his task, and the scrub herd took on an exotic look. Long ears here, a back hump there, and a pale blond cast crept into scruffy, brindle hides. But Autry became my nemesis. He had invaded my domain, and my fear of him cramped my peripatetic style.

Delano and I ran from the dead steer pen to his house. It was still early morning, and the family had gathered in the kitchen for breakfast after finishing the first chores of butchering day. The kitchen was joined to the main house by a dogtrot, where Mrs. Whatley made us wash our hands in a basin before we could eat. There was a long table in the kitchen covered with a green and white checkered oilcloth.

Mrs. Whatley, Sadie, and Ruby brought food—a large bowl of grits, a platter piled high with biscuits, a ball of churned butter, thick slices of salt pork fried crisp, milk gravy made from the bacon grease, rounds of sausage, a pitcher of frothy milk from the morning milking, cane syrup for the biscuits, and as many fried eggs as we wanted—from the wood stove to the table.

The Whatleys ate a lot, but they were all lean, thin people, except Sadie, who had plentiful breasts and round hips. The three boys, Wilson, Brock, and Cody, were handsome. They sang and played their instruments together, and like their father, they sometimes sang in church. All the girls were good-looking, but the youngest was especially pretty, and she sang solos in school. Delano's disgraced mother, Jessie, was the eldest daughter, and she never lived at home after he was born.

They all laughed a lot at their table, but their humor never amused me. They seemed to have a system of references that they all understood, and it took only a key word from one of them to send the others off into rounds of mirth. Sometimes Brock would make a sound like an enamored billy goat, and then his family would not recover for minutes. And they would laugh and exchange knowing looks and slap their thighs as many times as he did it.

Mr. Whatley, almost choking on his food and red in the face, would say, "Brock, you some show-out!" It didn't help to ask Delano why these things were funny, because he didn't know either. He laughed hard along with the others, but when I asked, he just shrugged his shoulders, rolled his brown eyes, and took another bite of his biscuit.

We ate as much as we could hold before we ran back out to investigate the butchering. It was early December and almost cold. I wore my overalls and a warm flannel shirt. Delano was dressed about the same, but he was barefoot. I bowed to my mother's insistence that I wear shoes to school and everywhere on cold days. We scuffed along the path to the barn.

The Whatley barn was a sensual, seductive place. A pungent scent hung everywhere in the barn, an epitaph to the sweet mixture of animal excretion there. And there was the smell of fresh milk, horse sweat, fermented straw, incubating eggs, sweet cow feed, chicken feathers, syrup, rats, and the soft bellies of kittens.

I loved kittens. The Whatleys kept dozens of cats in the barn to keep down the number of rats and mice. Most of the adult cats were timid, and some were downright wild. The males became territorial and fought. Sometimes the battles were so fierce, some of the cats were forced to abandon the barn and prowl feral in the pinewoods and hammocks, living on birds and rabbits. But there was usually a nursing queen in the barn tame enough to allow me access to her babies. And I would play with them and marvel at their sweetness and humor until someone forced me to go home.

The barn was also mysterious and scary. We weren't afraid of the big blacksnakes that slipped behind barrels and disappeared under straw as we entered the barn, their scales flashing in a shaft of light from the open door. We knew they wouldn't bother us. They were searching for corn rats, mice, and eggs. But sometimes we heard the staccato *whir-r-r* of a rattlesnake, and we knew we were in danger. Rattlers were timid and terrified of the blacksnakes, but when their food supply was scarce in the palmetto thickets and pine stands, they were forced to come to the barn to hunt. Delano taught me how to smell them. When we got a musky whiff of a rattler, we hurried outside to climb trees instead.

Delano and I could play in deep concentration in the cool, quiet barn for hours. On long summer afternoons we took our bags of marbles there and set up our ranches on the dusty dirt floor. We built little fences, corrals, and dipping vats for our herds of colorful marble cattle, which we drove, corralled, branded, and dipped. We supplied all the sound effects of the cattle drive ourselves. Delano was better at that than I was. He knew all the right terms, and when his horses ran to head off a steer, you could hear the hoof beats and the whips crack. And sometimes, he would cup his right hand under his left armpit and pump his elbow up and down to make the sound of a horse breaking wind. Then we would both laugh and roll on the ground with our cattle.

One afternoon when we were so engrossed on our hands and knees, heads close together over our herds, we suddenly felt a warm, silent splattering across our backs and over our heads, and when we sat back on our feet, we saw bright red drops on our cattle. We felt our heads, and when we looked at our palms, we saw that they were smeared with blood. Screaming, we ran through the open door and on to the house, leaving our cattle to fend for themselves.

We burst into the kitchen where Mrs. Whatley was leaning over her biscuit trough. She pulled the trough toward her flat abdomen. Her long face was flushed from the heat in the kitchen, and she brushed a strand of gray hair with the back of a doughy hand.

"Don't get none of that in my biscuits now," she said. We were both talking at once.

"It ain't nothin'," she said. "Just a ole owl up yonder in the rafters eating a mouse or a rat. From all that blood, I reckon it's a big rat. Now go out to the pump and wash yourselves off," and she began kneading her dough again.

Delano seemed satisfied with her diagnosis. But I felt somehow robbed by her mundane assessment of our bloody experience, and I determined to tell my father about this. I knew that I could count on him to come up with more exciting scenarios than Mrs. Whatley had offered. Comforted by that thought, I followed Delano out to the pump.

The barn nurtured an ecological orderliness. The cows, horses, mules, pigs, and fowl were fed by the Whatleys, who either ate them or otherwise took advantage of them. Aside from the vermin-eating cats and snakes, an enchanting array of other living things resided there and ate each other. Various species of spiders spun their lovely webs to trap insects, and high above the webs, mud-dauber wasps plastered their little round hogans securely to the walls along the eaves, singing mud-dauber songs and keeping beady eyes on the spiders. When the larval chambers in the hogans were prepared, the wasps attacked the spiders, injected them with a numbing anesthetic and carried them paralyzed, but living, up to their earthen nurseries. They tucked the preserved spiders into the waiting cubbyholes where they would become mother's milk for the pupae later on.

There were hundreds of miniature cone-shaped pits in the sand near the barn door. Concealed just under the sand in the bottom of each pit, tiny wolverine-like creatures lay in wait for a bumbling ant to slide into the funnel, and when that happened, the little demon under the sand rose up with a volcanic intensity and snatched the poor ant. Delano and I called them doodlebugs, and we squatted beside the pits and nudged ants over the edges to watch the sandy slaughter.

Shining, iridescent beetles, known as tumblebugs in Sweetgum Slough, sculpted marble-sized firm brown balls of cow dung and rolled them along, two bugs to a ball as large as themselves. Stumbling and falling on their backs and righting themselves over and over, they would continue rolling and struggling like two fat little drunks, out the barn door to some appointed hole in the ground outside. Usually, they made it there, rolled the ball down the hole, where they followed it and disappeared, safe in the underground darkness. But sometimes, a big puffy setting hen trotted up, famished, and pecked the weary insects into pieces, swallowed the glowing bug parts, and then had the dungball for dessert. Or from out of nowhere, a blue jay or a butcher-bird dropped down and carried the poor beetles up to a mite-ridden nest, bulging with red and yellow gullets.

The dead steers were gone when Delano and I went back to the pen. The older boys were preparing them for shipment to Dade City, where they would hang in the only refrigeration in the county. Delano's brothers sold their beef to grocery stores and kept some of it in storage for their own use throughout the year. And they used some for barter. In those days, both doctors in the county could be paid with a roast of beef or a good ham. The Whatleys butchered the hogs themselves. After rendering as much fat as they needed for lard, they stored the bacon, hams, and sausages in their century-old smokehouse.

Delano and I wandered to the back of the house where Mrs. Whatley did the family washing. She was bent over a work table in the yard. Two of the boys brought her a metal washtub full of hog intestines, and then they set another tub of fresh water next to it on the table. I peered over the rim of the tub to get a better look.

Mrs. Whatley plunged her strong, bony hands into the tub of intestines and began cleaning. Expertly, she squeezed the castings out between her thumb and forefinger. Then she pulled the length of gut inside out and threw it into the tub of clean water. She repeated this process without changing expression until she had been through the entire tub. She scrubbed and scrubbed, changed water, and scrubbed again until the offal was clean. In the meantime, she answered my questions.

"What are you going to do with them?"

"I'm going to clean them out so we can eat them."

"What is that stuff in there?"

"Ast your Daddy tonight when you go home. It's just the dirty part. The part we can't eat. You got to get rid of that, see?"

"Do you like to eat pig guts?" I called them guts because she did.

"Well, we don't eat them like this here. We get them real clean. We fix them up good. Ain't you never ate no chitlins or sausage? They the best part of the hog," she said, braiding three guts into a long pigtail and dropping it into a caldron of hot lard to deep fry. Her long narrow face squinted as she cooked.

Delano had drifted away after helping to build the fire for the caldron. I continued to skip around Mrs. Whatley and question her every move as she fried chitlins and stuffed yards of intestine casings with a mixture of her savory sausage meat. She let me stuff a length too and tie it into links, and together we went to the smokehouse, where she hung the sausages from hooks to cure among the ham and sides of bacon. And later, when we ate supper at the long table, she gave me cornbread flavored with crackling, the tasty residue produced by making lard. And she said I could take a pan of cornbread home to my mother.

After supper, Delano and I went back to the barn to make sure the chicken coops were all closed against coons, possums, and bobcats. We wandered on from there toward the pigpens, where the older boys and Mr. Whatley had slaughtered some hogs earlier that day. Delano stooped to pick something up. He scrutinized it as he held it in the palm of his hand. I moved close to him to get a better look at the thing in his hand. It was covered with dirt. Delano spit on it and rubbed it with his finger.

"I know what this is," he said, looking at me with his big dark eyes. "I seen one this morning when Cody cut a sow's belly open. They was a lot of 'um." He began looking around the ground for more.

"Well, what is it?" I stared at the soft, fleshy thing he held in his open palm. It looked like a dirty grubworm to me.

"It come out of a sow's belly when they cut her open." He lowered his voice, indicating that this was somehow a forbidden subject. "Cody told me they was baby pigs not borned yet."

I lowered my voice, too, in keeping with the gravity of the matter and the taboo now surrounding it. "Are you sure?" I whispered. Sometimes Delano took advantage of my trust in his knowledge and told me tall tales. "How do you know?" I asked.

"Cody said," he nodded. "Cody said they was."

"Well, it doesn't look like a baby pig. It's just a little dirty thing. I think it's a piece of hog gut." After all, I had recently become something of a player in the hog gut arena. He brushed some more of the dirt away and we both studied it again.

"See there? Ain't them little legs? It's a baby pig, all right. It just ain't growed. You want it?" He offered the gritty nugget to me, and I took it from him.

"Thanks," I said, holding it in the open palm of my hand with all the care it deserved.

The sun was disappearing through the live oaks and behind the barn. I saw my father's car turn into the Whatley property. He drove slowly along their grassy lane. Balder's mighty head lolled out of the back window. My father was coming to pick me up to save me from Autry.

"Here comes my father," I yelped, almost dropping the mystery in my hand. "I'm going to show it to my father." Holding Delano's gift in front of me as we ran, I had to shout over the sound of our pounding feet. "I'm going to show him. I'm going to ask him what it is."

We passed the dead steer pen, and their sad, dead song seemed far away now. We ran through the kitchen, where I could still smell chitlins and collard greens. We ran past the pan of cornbread intended for my mother and across the dogtrot and out of the front door. Breathless, we ran down the lane toward the car. I was running a little ahead of Delano. I had to look back at him.

"My father will know what it is." Delano caught up with me, and we ran side by side. The sun was gone, and we felt just a breath of winter air against our warm cheeks.

"If it's an unborned pig, my father will know. He'll tell us what it is. Come on!"

Lizzie

She stood predator-still beside me in the grassy rain ditch, ready to strike. Her skin, hair, and eyes—all the color of shallow bayou water—flowed together to form a single feature and give her the look of a well-planned reptile. Lizzie was my new friend, and I felt happy there with her in the hot, June sun, watching dozens of pale minnows taste our toes and ankles with their tiny soft lips.

"Them's good bait," she said.

I looked at her in surprise. I had not thought of the minnows as bait. I carried a small dip net and a Mason jar. Sometimes a rare marble fish or a red-tailed guppy appeared among the gray minnows around our feet. Then I would try to scoop it up and put it in my jar. But Lizzie could catch them with her hands. Like some nocturnal rodent, she would suddenly crouch down and snatch at the water in one successful, coordinated gesture. Then, smiling through missing teeth, she would release a wiggling specimen into my jar. I had to watch her closely, because she was just as adept at catching crawfish, small snakes, turtles, and other creatures capable of maiming my minnows. She had no fear of anything that swam or crawled. Lizzie, like the rest of her family, had learned how to survive in a startling variety of creative ways.

Her family came to the Sweetgum community in the early spring before school closed. Their strange little truck stopped at our front gate, and one of the children opened the gate so the truck could drive through. We were accustomed to seeing drifting families drive by, their old cars pieced together and loaded with children, dogs, and household items.

Those were the hard hours of the early 1930s in Florida when people, unemployed and hungry, left towns and cities to seek a bit of untended land where they could plant a garden and where it was wild enough to hunt and fish. Only a few of them turned into our driveway. When they did, it was to fill water containers or steaming radiators. Most were too polite to ask for food, but they were always hungry.

We watched this truck as it wound its way, rattling and bumping, down our rutted road until it stopped in front of our house. We were sitting on our front porch in the heat of the day.

My father stood up to greet a tall, tense man with an abdomen as flat as a tapeworm. When he got out and saw our big dog, he told the children to stay in the truck. Then he walked over to the porch.

"How y'all?" He wanted to know where he was and if my father had work for him. And he began to recite all the things he would be willing to do, which was everything he could think of, including hunting and fishing. And his wife could cook, he said.

My father explained that he already had a field hand and that we, ourselves, did everything else. The man nodded and was quiet for a long time, staring across our fields of young orange trees.

"Y'all know if they's ary empty house hereabouts?" My father suggested that he talk to a neighbor on down the road who would know more about things like that.

A baby cried. I jumped on the running board of the truck and looked into the passenger seat. A broad little woman sat there nursing a young baby. I called my mother to see, and the woman lifted a soiled blanket so we could see his face. I had never seen such a small human being, much less one feeding on his mother. She smiled at us and brushed a strand of thick, black hair from her face. I saw that her eyes were black, too, and as round as thumbtacks against her dark skin, which was oddly speckled with pinpoint, black freckles. She told us that the baby was only three days old and that he had been born in the back room of a filling station. She praised the filling station attendant's wife, who delivered the baby there on a day cot and who had given them all a meal before sending them on their way.

From the truck bed, three little girls peered at us from where they sat among pieces of furniture, washboards, tubs, cooking utensils, garden tools, and old mattresses covered with oil cloth. My mother told them to wait while my father and the man filled water containers at the pump. The children and I stared at each other fully. They whispered together behind cupped hands and laughed. I decided that I had been insulted, so I walked into the house where my mother was busy packing paper bags with staple food. She said that we would go to town tomorrow as she cleared our shelves of coffee, lard, flour, grits, and whatever canned goods she had on hand. And she found a clean, soft baby blanket somewhere.

They thanked us and drove away with the three little girls sitting in the back of the truck, their legs hanging down where a tailgate had been. I waved.

Two of them only stared back, but the other one raised her two hands to her face, stretching her mouth with her thumbs and pulling her eyelids down with her index fingers. I thought she looked good and ugly, which made me laugh. I figured she couldn't be all bad.

Several days later, the three girls came to school. Mrs. Cockshot introduced them as Martine, Elizabeth and Madeline DuLac. They looked silly, but I could tell they were scared. Their clothes and faces were clean, and the dirt rings around their necks were almost gone. During recess, Lizzie told me that they had found a house somewhere in the woods and moved in.

It proved to be the old McCracken homestead, long deserted and weather weary. I had seen it when I rode with my brother on his cowpony to the back prairie lakes where he liked to fish. Wall boards were broken or missing, the roof leaked, and part of the porch had caved in. The grounds were overgrown with dog fennel and thistles, and wild morning glory almost covered the house. Several great live oaks draped with Spanish moss shaded the yard. Outhouses were barely visible under vines and guava bushes. Two ancient crape myrtles in full bloom stood opposite each other on either side of the collapsed front gate, giving the eerie impression that someone might be at home.

I tried to imagine a family moving in there and setting up house, and I spent as much time at school as I could getting to know the girls who now lived in that old house. It was not easy, because they spoke with lisping accents, and when they spoke to each other, they used a language of their own. I soon called them by the names they called each other. Martine became Muttie, and Mut for short. Elizabeth, of course, was Lizzie. And Madeline was called Maddy. Mut was in the third grade, Lizzie was with me in second, and Maddy was in first grade.

Maddy's speech was so confused, I couldn't understand her at all. Mut was an unattractive, needy girl with coarse, straight hair and a reptilian aspect peculiar to her and Lizzie. But Mut's camouflage look was muddy rather than amber, and she was slow to react. The fact that she had large bosoms and the sullen, knowing look of a girl five years older than herself would have commanded respect from my second-grade classmates and me, even if she had worn a sign on her forehead that said "out of order."

Lizzie was bright and witty. As we became friends, she had an efficient way of knowing what I wanted, where to get it, and what to do with it. It was like having a handmaiden. As the youngest child in our family, I was used to fetching and accommodating, so I was attracted to Lizzie's willingness to supply my needs. But all three of the DuLacs were friendly and interesting and begged me to go home with them after school. My mother readily gave her consent. She was afraid of snakes and lightening, but she trusted people, especially those she didn't know.

After the first visit, I became a regular guest. As time went on, I took complete charge of the infant, whose name was Marvin and who was called Vinny. I bathed him in tubs of cold water while he screamed. I changed his diaper and carried him on my small hipbone, his unsteady head wobbling as I ran through the woods and fields with his sisters. This was a much better game than I played with my tomcat, Maxie, who was humiliated by wearing my doll clothes and riding in my baby carriage. In fact, I took my doll's entire wardrobe to the DuLac's house and spent hours dressing and undressing Vinny in pink organdy dresses and bonnets and hot woolen bootees until he fell asleep, either exhausted or in a coma.

I was intensely interested in this strange family whose mother went about barefoot on broad, flat feet and played wild games with us, even though her belly was still big and soft and her breasts leaked milk. Her name was Odile.

When I went home with other children from school, they had to change their clothes and do some chores before we could play. But Odile's home was unencumbered by expectation. Upon arrival there, I ran for the baby. The other girls ran to the trees to climb or to the tire swing. Odile and I became girlfriends, and she talked about things they did back home. Exciting things. Sometimes I thought my stories were uninteresting, so I embellished my trips to Tampa or summer vacations at the beach. Or I invented episodes that never happened at all just to entertain her and hear her laugh. If she suspected, she didn't let me know.

Mut liked to go to the kitchen and make iced tea laced with vanilla and laden with sugar. And she added slices of tiny limes and twigs of crushed mint from Odile's herb garden. Sometimes they even had ice, which they packed under a pile of sawdust at the foot of an oak tree in the shade. But we drank the tea barely cooled and without ice most of the time.

Odile and her husband had managed to free the house from vines and snakes and patch the walls and porch with boards that they took from an old smokehouse in the back. Odile spent hours cutting weeds in the yard with a sling hook, while sweat poured out of her body, from her shining black hair, and over her face. When the tallest weeds were cut and burned, she set fire to the rest, and cleared a large area around the house. They discovered a neglected open well, and it proved to have clear water after being cleaned of debris. Odile scrubbed the walls and floorboards inside the house, and she cleaned a rusting wood-burning stove in the kitchen. They opened all the doors and windows, and the house smelled less of rotting wood and stale air. With pieces of tin they acquired here and there, they patched the roof. Then they brought their few belongings inside and placed the mattresses on the floor of the bedrooms.

Their father's arrival was the highpoint of each day and the moment we waited for. Claude DuLac was a swamp man. He built a small pirogue, a tiny boat just big enough for him to stand in and pole his way through the still waters of the cypress swamps and small enough to secure to the top of his jitney truck. And with this matchbox vessel, he made a living.

In the spring, he gigged bullfrogs and sold them to elegant restaurants in Tampa. Risking his life, he robbed alligator dens of their long white eggs, brought them home and hatched them in a sunny nest he made himself of straw and sand. He covered them with chicken wire to protect them from robber varmints. Then on one of his bullfrog runs, he would take the beautiful and fierce little reptiles to Tampa where a man from Chicago paid him only enough money to buy some groceries and some ice on the way home.

He shot coons in the cooler months and stretched their skins on the walls of his front porch to dry before he sold them to a furrier. And in the dark waters of the swamp, he set long turtle lines that he baited with offal. Later, he would collect mud turtles, soft-shelled and yellow-bellied turtles and snappers. And sometimes he cast out into the still water among the lily pads, his rod and reel baited with lures he made by stretching frog skin over carved wooden plugs. Then he would land a fine mess of bass for their supper. He shot cat squirrels in the hammock lands and fox squirrels in the pine knolls, and he captured possums, which he caged in his yard and fed until they were cleansed.

And Odile knew how to butcher and prepare all of Claude's game with recipes passed down to her from her Native American and Cajun forebears. This she did with joy and a unique dash. Her daughters watched her and absorbed her enthusiasm and skill. Mut never grew tired of stirring a fine roux for her mother. Even the younger children learned how to pull the skin off a squirrel and scale fish. We all gathered around to watch Odile butcher a turtle. Sometimes when she cut the lower shell free from the carapace, eggs floated around in the bloody interior, and we let out a whoop of excitement. Just before the stew was ready to serve, Odile would drop the round eggs in like dumplings—some with soft white shells like dented ping-pong balls, but most were yellow yolks the size of marbles. All of them were succulent, simmered in the rich jus, seasoned with her mysterious herbs, and served up with chunks of tender meat and fresh vegetables. And there were always biscuits for sopping up the last streaks of gravy in our metal bowls.

Gigging bullfrogs or hunting alligators were nocturnal affairs, and sometimes Claude was out most of the night. Then he needed to sleep through the morning when the children were in school and while Odile cleaned the game or prepared the bullfrogs to sell. When he woke up, he drove the frog legs to market, because they were so perishable. But if he brought only alligators, Odile would skin them, cut roasts and steaks from the tails of the best ones and stack the valuable hides, while Claude lay under his truck tinkering with his tools. Occasionally Claude's swamp trips took him far from home, and he didn't return until the following afternoon.

Then the excitement would build. We wondered what mighty catch he was making and what we would eat for supper, and we waited for the choking sound of his little truck as it scratched its way through the pine woods and palmettos toward the old house. And there in the shade of moss-hung oak trees, it stopped, and we were all over it in seconds, marveling, touching scale and fin, fur and hide, looking into death-dull eyeballs.

With all the fervor of small carnivores, we hauled the game into the backyard where Claude had built a cleaning table between two trees. Odile scaled and gutted fish and Mut buried the entrails in Odile's herb garden. Turtles were placed in tubs of water, secure for future meals. Odile cleaned the squirrels and cut them into pieces. She scraped the skins and nailed them to the outside wall to dry. Then she dusted the squirrel meat with peppery flour and browned it in her big, black pot, where it simmered with herbs and onions on the wood stove. The wild aroma filled our heads and made our stomachs growl at us. The shining, sweating, joyful woman moved through Claude's cache of bloody animals as if he had just given her a pile of Christmas presents to open.

Mut made grits and biscuits. Odile poured a glass of moonshine whiskey for Claude and began frying fish in one of her heavy, black skillets. The tired man rolled a cigarette and sat at the long, crude kitchen table. Looking around him, he smiled at Vinny, who smiled back at his father from my lap.

"Hey, girl, you like that baby?" He spoke to me in a playful way, and I nodded. Maddy climbed in his lap and said something unintelligible. He sighed and sipped his whiskey, his day as complete as a full stomach.

During the meal they spoke their language together, and for the first time I asked Lizzie why they talked that way.

"It's back-home talk," she said. Then I wanted to know why they had left "back home," and looking into my face, her lizard eyes opening and closing, she said, "We had to. They made us." Odile gave her a sharp, warning look. I sensed a family secret. But it was a good enough answer between children. I had to go home.

Lizzie and her sisters said they would walk most of the way home with me, and Odile said she would come too. I told them that I was afraid of wildcats, and Claude laughed and said, "They's worst thangs than bobcats."

We left Claude holding Vinny and went outside. The sun was low, but the earth still shimmered from the heat of the day. I sniffed the air, which clung to the faint smell of entrails, blood, fur, and fish heads. It was their family scent, and I loved it. I walked away from the house with them on the trail left by Claude's truck.

As I held Odile's rough hand, I remembered all the things I had seen it do that day. Lizzie ran around and took my other hand, and we followed the trail to the hardroad. I felt wise and accomplished and in good company. And I was learning to look at almost anything with a view to eating it.

The Hardroad

It was an animal trail in the days when panthers stalked the slender deer and when black bears swung along with nothing particular on their minds. And it led Indian children to the blackberry patches where they filled up on the sweet, dark fruit that turned their tongues and white teeth purple. Tender pokeweed grew along the trail and offered itself up to laughing black-haired women who picked the young leaves and made a treat for their families.

The trail ran straight through the little hamlet that new white settlers named Sweetgum Slough. And those unyielding people from the hills to the north added a rut to the trail so they could get their horse teams and wagons through hostile palmetto thickets and dense hammocks. The crude new road curved around live oaks and ran through pine stands, sand flats, and shallow streams all the way to Brooksville.

I don't know when they paved it with asphalt and gravel and made it the hardroad. I don't know who labored on it or who paid for it. But it became the narrow gray nerve line of Sweetgum Slough, where horse-drawn buggies and carts took early settlers to San Antonio, Brooksville, and Dade City. And in time, little black automobiles ran along the hardroad and rattled over the wooden slough bridge, carrying people to remote rural towns where they would buy animal feed, chewing tobacco and snuff, get marriage licenses, have a tooth pulled, or go to the doctor.

By the time we moved to Sweetgum Slough in the early 1930s, the hardroad had suffered potholes and washouts and President Roosevelt's New Deal government employed local men to repair the road with more hot asphalt and gravel. People whispered around and said that the same men dug holes in the road at night so there would be work for them the next day. But that was probably not true, although Old Stitch said he saw Buck McCracken and Deke Crawley heading for the hardroad one night with shovels and pickaxes. My father laughed and said that those two were just on their way to a moonshiner's meeting. And he was right. People were desperate, but most of them were religious, honest, and law-abiding, as long as those virtues didn't interfere with an unwritten right—like the right to make whiskey.

The hardroad was the way to everywhere. It could lead us to Tampa to see a picture show starring Shirley Temple with her pouting mouth and bouncing curls, or Jeanette MacDonald keening to Nelson Eddy, who looked appropriately alarmed. It could take us to Brooksville to attend a county fair and ride a merry-go-round and stare at fat hogs and tiny, puffy chickens with feathered ankles or to be transfixed by a ghostly white peacock that strutted down the runway in pompous display and with studied grace, turned in slow motion around and around to offer us the full and dazzling vision of his miraculous, unfurled tail.

In the moonlight, the hardroad was a glowing satin ribbon that separated charging regiments of bayoneted palmettos and lighted our way to a *shivaree* as the whole Sweetgum community of men, women, and young children crept along on all fours, silent as a band of migrating crabs, to surprise old George Bailey and his new bride on their wedding night.

The hardroad's narrow shoulders sloped gently down to shallow rain ditches where amber water stood still and provided a sun-warmed home for minnows, salamanders, frogs, crawfish, turtles, and snakes. And thin black water striders skated on the invisible surface skin, feeding on wiggletails while damselflies clung to slender stalks of grass and watched with bulging blue eyes. And microscopic hookworm larvae waited below for our bare feet when we waded into the water with our Mason jars and dip nets. Then they burrowed into the skin between our toes, giving us fiery groundlich before traveling on through our bloodstreams and attaching themselves to the walls of our intestines. They sucked our blood and grew and made us pale and listless until Dr. Thistlethwait ordered us to swallow a pill as big as a quail's egg.

From my window at school, I had a good view of all activity on the hardroad. I could see the dour postman, Mr. Williamson, drive up and fill our mailboxes and then drive away, still dour. To Mr. Williamson, the hardroad was only Rural Route 1.

Every day at eleven o'clock, I watched the grand arrival of Malachi, a dignified black/Indian man, sitting aloof and erect on his handsome buggy pulled by a high-stepping horse. His boss lived in Tampa and raised fine horses in Sweetgum Slough, leaving Malachi in charge. Malachi would collect his boss's mail, turn the buggy around, and spin off back down the hardroad looking straight ahead, his profile like the Indian nickel, but where a feather might have been, Malachi wore a black Bowler hat.

And from my window, I sometimes saw Autry pass by, his hooves clicking on the gravel pavement, his huge head nodding as he stumped along with one of his goals in mind. The great white Brahma bull moved at large around the neighborhood. He liked to change his venue for several reasons—new concubines, greener pastures, and shade—and when he did, he walked smart and with purpose. I watched him from my window until he was out of sight. It was important to me to know where he went. Wherever it was, I knew that I would not wander there after school.

At night, raccoons and possums crossed the hardroad with their young, back and forth, looking for crawfish and frogs in the shallow ditches. Then cars with dim headlights came along and ran over the foraging rodents, leaving their carcasses to bake on the hardroad in the hot morning sun while bands of black vultures loped around in a floppy, macabre dance, pulling strips of red flesh and wet fur from the carrion until only the skeletons remained. Before noon, scavenging dogs carried the bones home to gnaw in the shade of a porch or under a house. And the hardroad was clean again.

My parents loved the hardroad in the moonlight. My mother was afraid of snakes, and she knew that they hunted at night, but her longing to be out under a full moon was greater than her fear, and she would go down our lane with my father to walk on the hardroad. Although rattlesnakes crawled in the darkness and lay in wait on the road to prey on young coons and possums, my mother felt safe because snakes were easy to see there. Sometimes, our whole family went to the hardroad to walk under a big white moon. Laughing and talking, we would walk too far, and my father would have to carry me back on his shoulders while our Great Dane zigzagged ahead of us, his hound nose to the ground.

The hardroad was a magical thing. As needed, it could change its character in the flash of a windshield, the blink of a goat's eye, or the crack of a whip. It brought the magnificent and terrifying person of Mrs. Cockshot to school each morning. Or it gave direction to a cattle drive when the Whatleys rounded up their animals at dipping or butchering time. In a thunderstorm, it guided panicky goats to the whitewashed church where they jumped through the open windows and left little brown marbles on the benches and in the aisle. It took the DuLacs away from me into the mist, and I never saw them again.

I did not know then that the hardroad would become a state of mind. That it would sometimes be a small, odd feeling in my body—like some familiar and not unfriendly thing left there by mistake after surgery. I didn't know that I would feel it as a stray blood vessel in my heart that suddenly throbbed when there was moonlight on the pine needles, when I heard a mindless chicken sing, or when I smelled the soft scent of a summer rain.

Or when I saw my father's blue eyes in my son's face.

Saved

Mrs. Cockshot couldn't keep her mind on the schoolroom. Standing beside the main door, she could see the tabernacle unfold in the field across from the school, and she could see Mr. Whatley direct the process and wave his arms about in an authoritative manner. He put himself in charge of community activities and spent his time attending to what he believed to be his duties. He appointed himself as a one-man school board, which gave him a prestigious role in the neighborhood as well as legitimate access to Mrs. Cockshot. Unfortunately for Mrs. Whatley, her sons encouraged these pursuits so they could run the family farm and tend the cattle without their father underfoot.

Mr. Whatley looked important out there among the palmettos, supervising the raising of the tabernacle tent in preparation for the big revival. He believed this event was sure to be one of his finer moments, and he wanted to be visible from the outset. For days, he had ridden his horse from house to house, informing Sweetgum dwellers about the revival and telling them how he had located the best traveling preacher in Florida to conduct it. He found my father tending his seedlings on our hammock property, and he left there only a few minutes later under the impression that my father planned to send Balder to the revival. Undaunted, Mr. Whatley moved on from neighbor to neighbor, like Paul Revere before the English.

We children used any excuse to get out of the schoolroom and onto the playground where we could get a better view of Mr. Whatley and his tent. We drank dippers of water from a bucket out by the well. From there, we could get a good look at the scene, and we stayed there as long as we dared, drinking and watching. Later, of course, we needed to go to the privy, which was down a long, winding path through the pines and palmettos. By walking backward, we had a fine view of the raising of the tabernacle.

As usual, I met Belle in the privy. We didn't bother to sit on the holes but rather stood peering around the door of the privy at the activity across the road.

"You know what, Biddy? I'm agoin' to that there 'vival meetin' tonight. Mama said they goin' to roll and speak in tongues. I'm agoin' to get Eulice to take me. You want to go with us?" Belle called me Biddy, because she said I was a little crybaby. And she was right about that. I cried when I burned my behind on the school stove, when other children hit or teased me, or when I missed my mother. I cried when I wasn't chosen for a team, and when Mrs. Cockshot whipped a child. I cried, not out of sympathy, but for fear I would be next. I cried when my current best friend rejected me for someone else. And Belle, like all the country children, couldn't pronounce my real name.

I wanted to go to the revival meeting with Belle and her young sister-in-law, but I didn't know how to go about it. I knew that no one in my family would go. My father found any form of religion amusing at best. My mother was still struggling to free herself from the Baptist cocoon woven around her with so much skill and fear by her mother and grandmother. I doubted that I could talk either my brother or sister into taking me. They were always busy with their own ideas and projects, and I was too afraid of wild animals to go out alone at night. But Belle saw the whole problem in one of her intuitive moments.

"Eulice and me will come git you on the way there and walk you home when it's done." Eulice, after all, was going on fifteen and pregnant. My father figured she would be motivated enough by her little round belly to keep out of harm's way. And she would be too afraid of her big, wild husband, Bird Dog, to do anything more than crouch on the hard benches in the tabernacle with all the other matrons, young and old.

We left my house at night, and the moon was shining. Belle and I scuttled like a pair of little raccoons ahead of Eulice down the rutted road that led from my house to the school. Balder rose from his place on the front porch and produced one questioning "woof" as we disappeared into the shadows under the pines. Belle and I held hands and slung each other around, fell down, and shrieked, loving our freedom in the moonlit night.

Eulice called, "Don't y'all git too far, now. Y'all got to hush up! They gonna thow y'all out makin' all that racket."

We paid no attention to her at all and ran straight up to the opening flap of the big tent, which had already begun to fill. Women and children sat on benches, their faces glowing pale orange from the light of the kerosene lamps placed on tables along the canvas walls of the tent. Men stood in the darkness outside, rolling and smoking cigarettes, chewing and spitting tobacco, and talking to each other in the undulating cadence of their gentle dialect.

Belle grabbed my arm and pointed, "Look yonder at that ole Arla Frady! What she think she's adoin'?" My eyes followed Belle's pointing finger to where our classmate, Arla, stood on the other side of the tent. Her expressionless, blue-eyed face stared back at us. But she had more important business on her mind. We watched her walk around among the men, tugging at their sleeves as they came into the tent to find seats.

We made our way toward Arla, pushing through the crowd like water bugs, Belle charging ahead with me in her wake. I stepped hard on Mrs. Whatley's bony foot, and she cried out in pain. I felt awkward and hateful, but in the heat of the moment, I couldn't think of anything to say, so I stared at her. Her body was like a long bent board, always leaning over something she was doing. When I went home with Delano after school to play, she leaned over us and gave us syrup bread to eat. She leaned over her kitchen table and over her stove and washtub. She let Delano and me put all the baby barn cats in her bed where we played with them until the time came for me to go home. I loved her for that. At last, she saw in my face that I was sorry I hurt her foot. She gave me a kindly pat, and her thin lips dragged an unconvincing smile across her white false teeth.

By the time I caught up with Belle, she had already accosted Arla. Hands on her hips, her face less than an inch from Arla's, Belle demanded, "Why you apullin on them men?"

Arla drew back, her face blank. "They got to be saved tonight. I'm atellin them they got to come to Jesus."

Belle, still on the attack, shifted from one foot to the other and changed the position of her hands on her hips. "Who says they got to? Jeeeesus?"

"Brother Harley Speed says. He ast me to tell the men to come to Jesus." Arla was a fair child with rosy skin, light eyes, and a shining blond helmet of hair, but what might have been radiant beauty was replaced by the waxen look of a stunned angel. Men gazed down at her over their tobacco-stained teeth or lower lips bulging with snuff and politely edged away toward their wives and relatives. Belle and I watched her as she moved outside the tent to where the real challenges were still smoking and spitting and probably nipping.

"That little turd! I wisht one of them men would kick her right in her booty!" With that, Belle flounced over and flopped down on the aisle end of a bench, patting the place beside her for me. I joined her and we both craned our necks to see what was happening up front. Mr. Whatley appeared, looking flushed and nervous. He stood behind Brother Harley Speed's portable pulpit and cleared his throat several times. Then someone handed him a glass of water. He took a swallow and made a long, numbing speech, giving himself elaborate credit for organizing the revival, which was sure to change our lives forever. He cleared his throat again and swallowed some more water. He was getting ready to sing.

Brother Harley Speed traveled fully equipped with a small organ and an old woman called Sister Iola Maude as organist. She hit a few tormented chords on the organ. Mr. Whatley tilted his head back, closed his eyes, opened his mouth, and sang, "Love lifted me. Love lifted me. When nuh-uh-thing else could help, love lifted me."

Belle gave me a poke in the ribs with her elbow. "Love lifted him, alright." Then with her hand over her mouth, she flashed me her most lascivious sidelong glance. I put my hand over my mouth, too, and we went into a fit of laughter as we pictured Mr. Whatley and Mrs. Cockshot being lifted by love.

Mr. Whatley sang "The Old Rugged Cross" and "What a Friend We Have in Jesus," and he invited the rest of us to sing the last one with him. Belle and I sang at the top of our lungs, as we had been taught to do by Mrs. Cockshot. Then Mr. Whatley introduced Brother Harley Speed, who stood up and approached the pulpit. He was a tall, rancid man in his early fifties with heavy, unwashed hair and dark rheumy eyes under swarming brows. He wore an old brown suit and a stained tie.

"It's mighty fine to be here in Sweetgum Slough tonight," Brother Speed began. "As I like to tell folks, I wasn't born in Sweetgum, but I come pretty close't. My daddy was a travlin' preacher like me. They was five of us chiren. I uz the oldest, and we uz born in five differnt places. My mother used to say she had her first pain in Sweetgum Slough and her first baby in Lutz." Brother Speed waited for laughter, which was not forthcoming. He moved on. "Well, I can see the Lord give me some good folks tonight. Some real good Christian folks." He allowed a weighty pause while he studied us. Then he added, "And I think the Lord give me some other folks who need to know Jesus Christ as their Lord and Savior. Am I right?"

Murmurs of "Amen" went through the tent. A few hands waved, and Mrs. Whatley sobbed into her handkerchief. I thought she was crying about her foot, but Belle said it was because Mr. Whatley and Mrs. Cockshot were lifted by love. And we started laughing again until Brother Harley Speed looked in our direction and frowned.

He walked around his pulpit and stood closer to the silent gathering. His voice was low and confiding. He was like an old friend who had dropped by with some choice and intimate gossip.

"I want to tell y'all, they's folks out chonder thinks they can git by without the Lord Jesus. I'm astin' y'all to think about that, now." He gave us a twisted, bitter smile, and his eyes slithered around the tent to see if we were thinking. Then he continued in a barely audible voice. "They hook up arms with Satan and march along with their backs to Jesus Christ right up to the doors of Hail before they know where they at!"

I hooked arms with Belle. Brother Speed shook his head like one in total disbelief, turned his back to us and faced his pulpit. Suddenly, he let out a hoarse scream, which ran through our bodies all the way to our gizzards. He began pacing back and forth across his stage like a tall, starved gorilla, panting and wailing. Pale faces, glowing in the dim lamplight, stared back at him, lips parted.

Brother Speed raged on. He threatened us with a colorful variety of castigations for our sins of bootlegging and drinking'liquor, smoking and chewing tobacco, lusting, lying, and being worldly. He told us that the flames of "Hail" were licking at our toes, that Satan was waiting to give us our fiery reward, and that all of this unpleasantness could be avoided if we would just walk down the aisle, come to Jesus, and know the "glowry" of the Lord.

Sister Iola Maude forced a mighty belch from the organ. Brother Speed wiped his face with a towel, and Mr. Whatley lifted his arms and sang, "Juh-ust as I a-am with-ow-owt one plea, I cuh-um dear Lord, I come to thee." Even his guttural, goat-like voice was a relief from Brother Speed's ranting. Belle and I watched Arla Frady, who was engaged in a frenzy of activity. Her numb face seemed at odds with her busy hands, tugging at sleeves, overall straps, and shirt collars. The men looked like large chunks of bait as she nibbled at them with her fingers and told them to come to Jesus. They seemed uncomfortable, but they stood their ground until she moved on.

At last, Bessie McCracken stood up, neck forward, head and eyes lowered, and started up the aisle. A few people nodded their approval. Bessie's thick, dark hair fell over her face. She sneaked furtive glances right and left as she proceeded, moving with the rhythm and bovine grace of a heifer, toward the pulpit where Brother Speed stood, looking more like an exhausted buzzard than a messenger of the Almighty. She caught sight of her cousin, Eulice, and broke into a demented adolescent giggle. I could see black hair on her stocky legs, and her rounded buttocks rose and fell under her skirt as she passed by Belle and me on her way to salvation.

Belle cupped her hand over my ear and whispered, "Bessie does it with everybody. She done it with two of my brothers, and she done it with J.T. Dawkins, too."

I didn't know what Bessie had done with JT and the Boggs brothers any more than I knew what Mrs. Cockshot was supposed to be doing with Mr. Whatley or what Belle claimed to do with various partners in the palmettos. But I pretended to know. I admired Belle for good reasons, and I wanted to appear to be as savvy as she was. So I drew in my breath, rolled my eyes, and asked her how she knew about Bessie.

"Eulice told me. Bird Dog told Eulice, and Eulice told me."

When we looked up again, the aisle was filled with people shuffling up to be saved. Mr. Whatley was still singing "Just as I Am," people were waving white handkerchiefs at the pilgrims, and Mrs. Whatley continued to weep. Belle turned to me.

"Come on, Biddy. Let's us go, too." She took my hand, and I jumped off the bench and followed her up the aisle toward Brother Harley Speed. I felt fear-thrilled, as though I were about to ride a Ferris wheel or jump into a deep swimming hole or climb over a fence where a bull was grazing. We pushed our way to the front of the group of penitents and found ourselves standing directly under Brother Harley Speed. We could look up into his nostrils and see that they were stuffed with hair.

"You little younguns, don't git so close in here, now." His voice was low and filled with irritation. "Just back up so we can git some room here." We backed up. I told Belle I thought Brother Speed didn't want to save children.

"I don't care what Brother Speed wants. I'm astayin'." So we stood firm while Brother Speed prayed for us, and we promised to accept Jesus. It was a long, tiring prayer, and I began looking around for a suitable distraction.

I saw Arla Frady standing a few steps away holding her father's sleeve as though it were a dog's ear. That was, indeed, an accomplishment. Frank Frady was the most innovative moonshiner in the county. He had done time in the state penitentiary twice, and after each incarceration, he came home to Sweetgum Slough with fresh ideas and ever more creative sites for his operation. My father smashed one of Frank's stills on our own property within weeks of Frank's second liberation. Undaunted, Frank returned to the wrecked scene and collected whatever items remained intact. He was a youthful man with a sweet smile and perfect white teeth that looked as though they tasted good. Smooth, tanned skin ran through his golden eyebrows into a white-blond hairline. Unlike his expressionless daughter, Arla, whose fine features were a gift from her father, Frank Frady's lively being shone through all the apertures of his handsome face. Glittering, aquamarine eyes viewed his world with amused good humor.

Belle looked at Frank and said, "Ole Frank's just tryin' to make folks think he ain't agoin' to moonshine no more."

Brother Speed raised his hand at last and told the reborn to remain with him until the congregation left the tent. There was more to come. At his signal, Sister Iola Maude attacked "Onward Christian Soldiers" with the organ. Mrs. Whatley stood at the opening of the tabernacle, leaning over the shiny metal syrup can in her scrawny hands. Those who could afford to dropped coins and even a few dollar bills into the can for Brother Speed. Then they filed out of the tent into the night.

Mr. Whatley and Sister Iola Maude began to move the organ and the pulpit against the tent walls, and they pushed benches back to make room in the front. They emptied several large bags of sawdust on the ground and Mr. Whatley spread it around with a rake. When the scene was prepared, Brother Speed asked us to gather around him. I saw Eulice still sitting in the back of the tent. Her little round face looked tired. And I could tell that she was exasperated with Belle and me for getting saved.

Without warning, Sister Iola Maude let out a series of yelps. Her eyes swiveled back into their sockets, her old body stiffened, and she fell into the sawdust almost face down. The sound that came from somewhere deep in her throat was like nothing any of us had heard before. Then she began to roll around in the sawdust, first in one direction and then in the other.

Belle said, "Shit. I can do that easy. First me and then you."

Belle was about to make her move when Bessie McCracken went down with a thud, like some kind of muffled explosion, hairy calves flailing the air and kicking up sawdust. Her big green eyes fluttered and she made a gurgling sound. Next Frank Frady plunged, scooping sawdust in front of him as though doing the breast stroke. I looked at Arla, who was observing her father with all the exuberance of a garden statue, wide blue eyes coldly fixed on his progress. Frank twisted and rolled, sawdust inside the bib of his overalls and sticking to his face where some spittle had escaped during his downward spiral.

Belle and I were transfixed watching Brother Harley Speed and his followers. They dropped beside us, in front of us, and behind us. Brother Speed's excitement mounted.

"The spirit of Jeeesus is in you!" he shouted. "Give up to the Lord." He fell to his knees in the sawdust, hands clasped and face toward Heaven. Then he rolled over on his side like a stiff old football player. Suddenly, Belle went down, eyes wide open, and rolled into Brother Harley Speed who gave her a push. "Move over, youngun."

Belle obliged. She rolled over and over, like a fast little keg. Then she rolled back. As she passed the spot where I stood gaping, she motioned with a crooked finger for me to follow. The sawdust felt good and smelled good. I set my course and rolled in Belle's direction. She howled a few times like a young hound at bay while I tried to imitate Bessie's gurgle.

As I rolled past Sister Iola Maude, I saw that she was sitting up. She looked dazed as she dug sawdust out of her bosom. Sarah Floyd rolled by me in a blur of bright red, greasy lipstick and flying brown hair. Several glottal clicks came from her throat.

The sights and sounds around me were strangely exhilarating, and I found that I could gurgle, click, moan, and yelp with abandon. Belle and I rolled together. We rolled in opposite directions. We rolled back together and bumped heads. Belle did a complete somersault over her back, legs over her head. She sat up and shook sawdust from her bushy hair. I pulled up beside her. Glowing, she leaned toward me in the way she did when she had some urgent obscenity to share with me.

"You just watchie ole Brother Speed. He's got his eyes wide open when he rolls so he can look up Bessie's and Sarah's dress." I looked for Bessie. She was lying spread-eagle, staring at the ceiling of the tent. Just below her, Brother Harley Speed was lying on his belly, his cheek resting in the sawdust, burning eyes staring ahead.

Belle whispered, "Roll over yonder, and you'll see what he's alookin' at." I did a one and a half spin, put my cheek in the sawdust and found myself staring straight into Bessie's dark, mellow crotch.

I rolled back to a triumphant Belle.

"I told you so," she said.

Brother Speed, having satiated himself for the moment, rolled over a couple of times until he spotted Sarah. A quiet had fallen over the new Christians. I heard someone say, "Praise the Lord," and someone else emit one last primordial gasp. Belle pushed me, and we both inched forward on our elbows like commandos until we could observe Brother Harley Speed's revised view. Sarah lay on her side in a fetal position, knees drawn up to her ribs. But her skirt in the back was furled around one shoulder, exposing a soft buttock cheek. Bright pink underpants disappeared into her cleft like a G-string. Brother Speed lay panting, eyes partially closed, face toward the vision. Belle and I studied this scene as though it were a fishing cork about to go under. I waited for Belle's comment.

"Brother Speed's agoin' to git him some tonight." She nodded gravely. Then the preacher dragged himself to his knees. Sister Iola Maude, having played her role, went to the organ, sat herself down in front of the instrument, and played "I'm Saved, Hallelujah." Everyone sat up in the sawdust. Frank Frady took out his tobacco can and cigarette papers, but Arla snatched them from his hands before his fingers could begin their familiar routine. Brother Speed smiled at her and told Frank that Arla was his guardian angel.

Belle said, "I hate that little chicken shit, Arla." I decided that I hated her, too, and hugged Belle.

Brother Speed turned to his new flock and said that he needed to talk to us about our reborn life in Jesus and that we should come to him, one by one, before we left the tent. I heard Eulice sigh. She stood up and held her back with two hands. Then she yawned and went outside to wait for us. Frank Frady met with Brother Speed first in the back of the tabernacle. They had a short, serious talk, and I heard Brother Speed say, "God bless you, son."

Frank gave Brother Speed some moonshine money. Then he and Arla left together.

Next, Sarah Floyd and Brother Speed had a talk. Belle and I watched closely. We saw Sarah give him a wan little smile with her red mouth. Brother Speed offered her a handkerchief, and she wiped all the sinful lipstick off, returned the handkerchief and left. I looked at Belle. She shook her head.

"He ain't gittin' none from her."

Several more souls were blessed before they paid up and walked out into the darkness. Mr. and Mrs. Whatley left with Sister Iola Maude, who had been given a bed at their home for the week of the revival. Finally, Bessie McCracken moved forward, beating some sawdust from her rump. Then she sat down awkwardly by Brother Speed. Like a goodly priest, he cupped his two hands around her face and spoke to her. She nodded. He leaned forward and whispered in her ear. Her green eyes opened wide. He whispered in her other ear. She snatched a look around her, giggled, and left.

Belle and I strode up to Brother Speed together. He looked at the two of us.

"You little younguns understand what a glowrious thing happened here tonight?"

Belle let him know that she understood very well what had happened. I nodded. We each gave him a nickel, hung on to each other, and met Eulice outside the tent. She marched down the road ahead of us, holding her hard little belly like a basketball that she was about to pass to a teammate.

Suddenly, Belle stopped. She took my hand and we ran back toward the tent. Belle pulled me behind the big oak tree in front of the school.

"Now, just watchie," she whispered. Out of the shadows, the lumpy silhouette of Bessie McCracken reentered the tabernacle just before the kerosene lamps inside went out. Belle took my hand, and we ran howling down the hardroad behind Eulice, skipping in big strides. Belle sang, "I told you so! I told you so! Ole Brother Harley Speed's agoin' to git him some tonight!"

Eulice said, "Y'all shut up!" And I was delivered, as promised, to my door.

My father sat reading at the dining table where he had a special, powerful lamp. My mother sat across from him, working an algebra problem that had obsessed her for days, while the food went uncooked and the beds went unmade.

I hopped onto my father's lap. He asked me what had happened at the tabernacle. I told him that Mr. Whatley had sung "Love Lifted Me" and that Belle and I had laughed because of Mrs. Cockshot and Mr. Whatley. I told him Belle said Arla Frady was a chicken shit and that we both hated her. I listed everyone who was saved including Belle and me. I told him how we rolled and spoke the unknown tongue and that Brother Harley Speed looked up girls' dresses.

When I told him how Frank Frady tried to roll a cigarette right after being saved, I had to speak with increasing force to be heard above my mother's laughter. And I kept the best for last. Then I told him about Bessie McCracken sneaking back into the tabernacle, and I ended by quoting Belle. "Ole Brother Harley Speed's going to get him some tonight."

"Great God Almighty!" said my father.

Purple Socks

Balder's sudden bark exploded into our sleep like a hand grenade. My sister and I lay breathless and rigid in our bed, listening to our father's footsteps as he hurried to the front door with a flashlight. Someone was pounding on the door, and Balder went into a vocal frenzy. We heard my father issue sharp commands to the big dog, and then we heard him open the door.

"You can come in. Come on in. I've got him. He won't bite you while I'm here. What's the matter?" My sister and I peered around the door of our bedroom and saw a man come in out of the night into the beam of my father's flashlight.

"It's my little youngun. The boy. He's went out of his head. I'm scared he ain't goin' to make it." The man's voice broke. "Edna thought maybe could your wife come help us."

We stood around in our nightclothes listening to Dewey Gresham as he delivered his message, pale and shaking. He had walked miles through the woods to get to our house. My mother lit a kerosene lamp while my father restrained Balder, who was still not convinced that Dewey was an acceptable visitor. It was three o'clock in the morning and cold.

My father was not a sociable man in the Sweetgum community nor was he arrogant. He was not a southerner, and he lacked the southern mercurial gift for communicating at a variety of levels. He made little effort to befriend the local people, and he kept himself aloof from their problems and their pleasures. But he knew most of them by name, because at certain times of year he needed more help in the groves than Enzo Hendry could provide. Then he hired some of our neighbors for a week or two. So he recognized Dewey Gresham when the man came to our house that night.

My mother came forward with the lamp, and put it on the table in the dining area of our great room. She wore my father's old bathrobe which she found in the darkness of their bedroom. She looked even smaller than she was

42

as she motioned to Dewey to sit at the table while my father, still gripping Balder's collar, took the dog through the kitchen to the back door. My sister and I stood shivering in our pajamas in the doorway of our bedroom, watching our mother and Dewey where she joined the distraught man in the lamplight. Her long, dark red hair, released for the night from its chignon, rested on the table as she leaned toward Dewey to listen.

By then we had lived in Sweetgum Slough for two or three years, and my mother's reputation in a sick room was known throughout the community. Disputing her blithe, romantic, and almost lackadaisical manner, there were also formidable nuggets embedded in her as firmly as time capsules, which she could release on demand. And one of them was her ability to doctor and heal. Her own mother had had the same gift, but she expressed it in a way as different as the personalities of the two women.

Both mother and daughter had grown up around my great-grandfather who took his Yale medical skills to Florida from South Carolina to practice his craft in a tiny hamlet on the Manatee River. A quiet community, it had earlier been haven to many of his friends when they had been refugees or recovering from the terrible War Between the States.

At different periods in his long and respected career, both my grandmother and my mother accompanied the old doctor in his horse-drawn buggy to make calls and to assist him as he delivered babies, set broken bones, lanced boils, and treated the raging fevers of malaria, typhoid, and diphtheria. They rejoiced with him over his many successes, which he accomplished with the skill of his hands and the patience and stubborn dedication of his Baptist soul, without the help of miracle drugs. And they wept with him at the funerals of those who, despite his nights-long vigils, he was unable to save. When he died of injuries after his buggy slipped off a bridge in the rain, they grieved for him with all of Manatee County.

When my mother was old enough to accompany him on his calls, she found that doctoring came to her naturally, and she told her grandfather that she wanted to study medicine. But he was an old-fashioned, narrowly religious physician who believed that it was unseemly for women to go through the rigors of medical school beside men. When the time came for my mother to go to college, he convinced her parents that teaching was the only appropriate profession for a young lady of her standing. So they sent her to Brenau Teacher's College in Gainesville, Georgia, where she studied and became a good teacher. But her heart and her lifelong gift remained in healing.

In 1931, when we moved to the backwoods, there were two elderly doctors in the county. They were good men who traveled throughout the rural areas in their black Fords to treat the country people—the hard-pressed farmers who struggled to keep food on their tables and the depression at bay. They treated the hapless, wandering refugees who were at the mercy of the national impoverishment. The two doctors attended the poor with the same level of respect that they offered to everyone else. It was a good time to be young and forming. It was a good time to observe.

My mother often took Sweetgum patients to the doctors in our car. Or she went to town alone to fetch one of them on behalf of someone who was too ill to make the trip. Electricity had not been extended to rural areas of the county, so there were no telephones. Sometimes the busy doctors could not be found, and hours could go by before a patient was examined. And country folk delayed getting to a doctor until the sick one was beyond repair. They would try all of their home remedies and superstitions first, because they were either afraid of the doctor or too proud to ask for treatment when they were penniless—even though they knew that both doctors were kind men who would travel miles through the night in their sputtering cars to deliver a baby. When there was no money to pay him, people often gave the doctor's name to the newborn baby. It was done to honor the doctor. As a result, there were several unfortunate boys in the county who were called Thistlethwait, and one girl with a shortened version of the name and known as "Thissie."

As the doctors came to know my mother, they grew to trust her. She helped them in our neighborhood when there was a delivery, an epidemic, or a crisis, and they encouraged her to work on her own when her skills were needed. They trusted her to know her limitations and to know when to get a doctor.

While my mother dressed and organized her medicine box, my father made a pot of coffee. Dewey Gresham drank the strong brew and recovered some of his composure. Then he and my mother drove into the night in our car. We knew we would not see her again until she felt it was safe to leave the boy. And that could take days.

The child, Wiley, was in pain and delirious when my mother and Dewey arrived at the wood-frame house in the backwoods. Edna, his mother, a lumpy girl in her early twenties, sat beside him where he lay on the only bed in the house. Her plain face was flushed, and her eyes were red and swollen.

The two rooms of the house were warmed by a small iron stove, and the older child, Emmy, slept on a pallet behind it. The Gresham children were known to be sickly and regularly missed weeks of school. Most people in the neighborhood said that Dewey and Edna were lazy and careless parents. But my mother told my father that they were just young and ignorant.

My mother greeted Edna and sat in the chair beside the bed while the two young parents stood at its foot. Wiley lay whimpering and in a stupor. My mother touched his forehead with her lips. Then she took a rectal thermometer from her box, shook it down, and with gentle hands, she inserted it in his small behind. She washed her hands in a basin on the stove and rubbed Wiley's back to quiet him until she could remove the thermometer. His temperature was near 105 degrees. My mother was quiet and moved fast while the frightened parents watched. She asked Dewey to place a washtub of lukewarm water on the kitchen table. The man and his wife did as they were told while my mother examined the boy's throat and ears. His throat was inflamed, and one ear was sensitive. In a lucid moment he stared at her, and between sobs he told her that his ear hurt.

"Yes, I know. We're going to fix it," she said.

She undressed the boy, removing his dirty overalls and a ragged undershirt to expose his pitiful, bone-white small body. She gathered him into her arms as if he were an infant and lowered him into the washtub of water. His parents were alarmed, but they didn't interfere, and the small boy was too weak to protest. My mother knew that most country people never bathed more than faces and hands on a regular basis and sometimes an occasional neck or bottom. But an entire body was never submerged in water. She knew the young parents were frightened as she held the boy in the tepid water, rubbing his limbs and body and squeezing water from one of her washcloths over his forehead and cheeks.

"He has a high fever," she explained. "We have to get the fever down fast. The water will bring it down. Then we'll see what else we have to do." She continued bathing the child as his mind cleared and his body cooled, but he became more aware of the pain in his ear, and he whimpered like an injured puppy. My mother spoke soothing words to him while his parents looked on.

She dried him with a towel from her box and dressed him in one of my flannel pajamas and put him back in bed. She adjusted the crude pillow under his head and found there the inevitable bone-handled knife that country people believed would cut the fever and the pain. She didn't argue, but she handed the knife to Dewey and said, "His fever is down. He won't need this anymore. Put a kettle of water on the stove to boil." Then she covered Wiley's chest with a flannel cloth.

On the table by the bed she found bottles of foul remedies including a mixture of urine and kerosene that Edna had poured in Wiley's ear. My mother put them all in her medicine box so they could not be used again. Later, with warm boiled water and a syringe from her box, she carefully irrigated the infected ear until the abscess burst and drained, and the boy slept, free of pain and fever. She let him sleep for several hours while she sat beside him in the lamplight.

Edna gave my mother strong coffee to drink, and she fried slices of salt pork until it was crisp. Then she put the bacon in a large biscuit that she first slathered with grease, and she offered it to my mother, who enjoyed the tasty food after the long night.

At daybreak, Wiley woke up and looked around him. He had a big head for his small six-year-old body. Whispy ginger hair grew over his ears and his pale forehead. His brown eyes were dull from his ordeal, but he smiled, and my mother saw that most of his upper teeth were missing.

"How do you feel?" she asked.

"Froat huts," he answered.

"What about your ear?" she asked.

"Huts dis a litta bit," he said.

"Are you hungry?" she asked.

"Firsty," he said. My mother went to her box where she kept a bottle of grape juice. She poured some of it into a cup and gave it to him after she helped him into a sitting position. She spoke to Edna.

"He's going to need some soup. Can you make soup?" she asked. The girl stood there like a pile of dirty laundry.

"I ain't got nothin' but some beans and not many of them," Edna said. "Maybe Dewey can kill a rabbit or a squirrel, but I ain't got nothin' else to put in it."

She thought it was too much trouble to keep a vegetable garden, even the nutritious turnip and collard greens that were easy to grow and standard fare throughout the county. For the same reason, she didn't keep chickens or any other fowl, so there were no eggs either. The Greshams ate large quantities of grits, beans, fat bacon, and biscuits that were provided by the government relief program. Sometimes Dewey brought in small game and fish when he felt like it and when he had enough money to buy bullets. Dewey didn't like to work on the road for the WPA, so he rarely had money. And when he did, he bought tobacco.

"I'll go home now and make some soup," my mother told them. "I'll come back this afternoon to check his temperature and bring the soup. Keep him in bed. Give him grape juice as often as he will drink it. If you let him get up, the fever will come back. Here are some books for you to read to him." She handed Edna a small stack of my books from her box.

Edna giggled. "I can't read," she said.

My mother turned to Dewey. "Dewey?" she asked.

"I ain't never learnt neither," he said. "My daddy needed us in the fields. I never liked goin' to school nohow." He smiled and took the books from my mother.

"Then show him the pictures. Do whatever will keep him in bed." She leveled her gaze and looked as stern as she could. She had given an order, and Dewey knew it.

My mother went to the sick boy and sat by him again. She took his hand. "Wiley, I'm going to town this morning to get some things to make your throat feel better. You have to stay right in bed. And I'll bring you a present. Is there something you would like to have?"

The boy smiled. He had never had a present. He thought a long time and then he said, "Thocks."

"What color?" my mother asked, understanding him.

"Furfle," he replied. His eyes were almost bright. She felt his forehead with her hand and found it damp. The fever was gone, but she knew it could return in the afternoon. And she knew that another bout of high temperature could carry the frail, malnourished child away in the flutter of a falling leaf.

She came home and made enough soup for their family and ours, then she drove on to Dade City and bought the medical supplies she needed and a pair of bright purple socks. It was late when she returned, but she still had to take the soup to the Greshams, check on Wiley, and give him the socks she promised.

When she finally came home, we could see that she was weary and frayed—not by the activity of the day, but from the weight of living inside that other persona of hers. She walked down past Tony's stable in the twilight and followed the path leading to the pond.

"Where is she going?" I asked my father.

"She'll be back," he said.

"But why is she taking a walk in the dark?" I asked.

"Because she's a cat. She can see in the dark," he said. "She's going down there to watch ghost birds and things that come out of the night. Fairies and wampus woogles and a few fluggers." My father was setting the table.

It made me angry when he talked like that. "She is not," I wailed. "You're just teasing me!"

He laughed. "She's going down there to drink some magic pond water. When she comes back, she'll be a moon maiden with starfish in her hair."

"And you're a weirdwolf!" I hollered.

"Werewolf," he laughed, correcting me.

"You're growing long hairy ears and big warts." I yelled, getting into the game with him. He was pouring buttermilk into tall glasses.

I took a white glass in my two hands. "I'm going to throw this on you," I said. "I'm going to change you into a big white rabbit!" I stood my ground, the tall glass of buttermilk held out in front of me.

"Well, then," said my father, "I'll just have to pour this on you and see what you turn into." He took another glass of buttermilk and poured it on my head.

I stood there in disbelief for a moment, blinking through the buttermilk, little pieces of butter draining through my eyelashes and down my cheeks. My father leaned over, his eyes filled with blue mischief.

Though almost blinded by the buttermilk, I aimed well and got him full in the face with my glass of the thick milk. He sputtered and laughed and grabbed another glass of buttermilk, but I ran out of the kitchen and out of the front door into the darkness. When I came back, hoping he would be waiting to douse me again, he was in the kitchen with my mother. He was mopping the floor, and they were both laughing. My brother and sister were there, too.

We gathered around our table in the breakfast nook and began to eat our soup. My sister wanted to know what my mother had done in town.

"I bought some purple socks," she said. And that was all she said.

Death and The Hurleys

"God damn it!" My father's eyes seemed to be melting. I watched as his tears dropped crystal clear and heavy onto the white satin surrounding Bird Dog Boggs' dead face. Then he turned away from the coffin and stalked off through the churchyard in the direction of our front gate where Balder waited to lick his hands and cheer him up. My father had liked exuberant, unruly Bird Dog, but he cried often and about a wide variety of things. So I was not daunted by his tears as I took my turn to view Bird Dog's corpse.

I had never seen a dead human being. My experiences were limited to the parade of animals Claude Dulac gigged, shot, hooked, snared, or clubbed to death and brought home, their eyes open and glazed, mouths ajar, with blood oozing out, tongues lolling through sharp, yellow teeth. So the sight of Bird Dog was almost a pleasure. I expected to see him frowning, at least, or to be baring his white teeth in anger at the horse that had thrown and killed him.

Instead, he looked serene, his dark skin and black curls a compelling contrast to the white satin pillow that supported his handsome head. I studied the shape of his eyelids, thick, arched brows, and the long eyelashes resting on his tanned cheeks. His brown hands held the coiled, braided cow whip that he had made for himself.

I was trying to imagine what it felt like to be dead when Arla Frady tugged on my skirt and said, "It's my turn. You taken everybody's turns." Arla, the evangelist, with her halo of light hair and her blank face. She never succeeded in getting Bird Dog to come to Jesus. I took one last greedy look at the dead young man and decided I would ask my father someday about Heaven. I stepped down from the crate that had been provided for children and relinquished my place to Arla, who gave me an impious little shove.

I skipped down the aisle of the Sweetgum church toward the front door. The funeral service had not begun, although Mrs. Whatley had taken her place at the old piano, and the Boggs family was gathering in the front pews near the casket. I passed Eulice, Bird Dog's baby-faced, young widow, now sitting with her own family, the McCrackens. Her baby was due, and she looked pale and frightened as she sat holding her mother's hands. The air in the church was stale. Someone sobbed, and I wanted to be outside in the sunlight.

School was closed for the funeral, and it was a nice, fall day. In our part of Florida, fall and spring were hardly detectable seasons. Fall was cooler than summer and not as cold as winter. People prepared to grind sugarcane, make syrup, dip cattle, brand calves, treat screwworms, and butcher hogs. Children went into the pine woods and palmetto thickets to collect lighterd knots— odd chunks of aged wood used in cookstoves and prized for their lasting heat. My father and Enzo Hendry stacked firewood in the lanes between the rows of young orange trees in preparation for a possible winter freeze. Fall was a time when everyone felt a new flush of energy as they were relieved of the intense heat of summer.

Outside of the church, I saw Belle sitting under a tree. The one Mrs. Cockshot used to shade her car on school days. When I sat down beside Belle, she hugged her knees closer to her face and stared straight ahead. At last, she looked at me full-faced. Her features had lost all of their impudence. Even her hair was subdued.

"Biddy, I ain't goin' in there. You better go on by yourself." Her voice was hoarse. I asked her why she didn't want to go to her brother's funeral. "It's better out here," she explained. She watched a mockingbird fly out of the tree. "And I don't want to hear nothing about God." I asked her if she would like to come home with me to play. I told her we would play anything she liked. That was a dangerous commitment, but she just sighed, got up, and began walking down the hardroad toward her house. I watched her until she was out of sight.

Inside the church, Mr. Whatley was leading the congregation in "Jeez-us, like a Shepherd Lee-eed Mee-ee," and when I peeked in the door, I saw my mother sitting by herself in the rear of the church, and I was tempted to go back in and sit beside her. I had wanted to see them put Bird Dog into the ground, dirt and all, but I decided to leave. I walked out of the churchyard, past the school, and down the rutted road, trying to decide what to do. Everyone I knew was in church.

I stopped in front of the Hurley's gate to watch the chickens. The Hurleys had about twenty acres, a neat, sturdy house a little smaller than ours, and several small outhouses. They also had hundreds of White Leghorn chickens, scratching and pecking the ground as far as the eye could see. The old couple sold eggs in all the towns and hamlets of the area, and sometimes Mr. Hurley drove all the way to Tampa with a truckload of eggs. My mother used to buy eggs from Mrs. Hurley before she got her own Rhode Island Reds.

But no one really knew the Hurleys. I think they didn't want to be known. They were not local people, and they didn't mingle with Sweetgum folk. Catholics, they kept to themselves and tended their chicken farm and went to church in San Antonio on Sunday. As I stood there, Mr. Hurley came out of the house and got into his little truck. He drove down his long driveway toward the gate where I was standing. I quickly lifted the latch and opened the gate for him.

As he drove through, he stopped a moment and said, "Thank you, girlie. What you want out here? Where's your Mama at?"

I told him everyone went to the funeral. "Huh? Oh, that Boggs feller. Well, he's been askin' for thata one." I wanted to know if I could go to see Mrs. Hurley. He seemed surprised. "You want to see her? Just go on in there. She's out and around somers, I guess. I ain't seener myself for about three hours." He laughed. "That's a woman you don't miss even when she's there." He laughed again and drove away. I closed the gate, but I got myself inside first as I pondered his remark about his wife.

After searching the outhouses, I finally met Mrs. Hurley coming out of her back door. She was startled to see me.

"You the little girl from over yonder by the church and the school, ain't you." It was a statement. I nodded my head. "Well, what you doing over here in my yard?" I was becoming uncomfortable. I found it hard to tell her that I just wanted to look around the place and to know what she was like. So I told her that my mother sent me to borrow two aspirins. "*Two* aspirins? She got a sick headache?" I nodded again, not knowing what she meant. "Well now, I guess it's easier to send you for some of *my* aspirins than it is for her to go git some of her own."

I rushed to my mother's defense. "She can't, because she's got a broken arm."

"Broken arm, has she! How'd she break her arm?"

"She fell," I said.

Mrs. Hurley looked at me. "Young woman like that just fell?"

"I mean my father pushed her down," I said. Mrs. Hurley turned around. She had been heading for her kitchen door to look for aspirin. Her flushed face was suddenly alight with interest, the thin gray braid wound around her fat head seemed to tighten, and her crossed eyes bulged, enormous behind her thick glasses.

"Well, you come in here with me, and we'll get some aspirins. And you can have a biscuit with butter and syrup, too." Her kitchen was fresh and scrubbed everywhere. The linoleum on the floor shone, and the pungent scent of Octagon soap filled my head. She told me to sit down at the kitchen table, which was covered with green and red flowered oilcloth. "What would you like to drink with your biscuit?"

"Coffee, thank you, ma'am."

"Coffee! A little girl like you? How old are you anyways?"

"Seven. I always drink coffee with my father," I said. That was true.

"Well, I ain't surprised about that." Mrs. Hurley sniffed and tossed her head.

"The doctor in Tampa told us to drink coffee. It's good for our kidneys. My father only has one kidney." I thought that adding a fact would lend credence to my story.

"You goin' to end up with only one kidney too if you don't look out. Well, I'm agoin' to have a cup, and you may as well too, I reckon. What do you want in it?"

"Just black, please ma'am."

"Well, you got good manners, anyways." She sighed. She boiled the coffee and strained it though a sieve into our cups. She put a lot of cream and sugar in hers. Then she put a cold biscuit filled with butter and syrup in front of me. She squeezed her plump body into an armchair and rested her elbows on the table, holding her cup in both of her hands. I noticed that her hands were red from washing dishes and clothes and scrubbing floors. She stared at me behind her bulging lenses with her huge crossed eyes.

"Now why would a big ole feller like your daddy push a little woman like that?" I could tell that she was settling in for some choice baiting, so I felt compelled to accommodate her.

"He doesn't *always* push her *all* the way down." I took a big bite of the syrup biscuit to give myself time to organize my story.

"You mean, he's did it more than oncet?" Some biscuit stuck in my throat, and I needed time to sip the hot coffee and think. In the meantime, I nodded and swallowed hard.

"Well, he just does it when she gets in his way. Like if he's in a hurry to go out to the privy, or if it rains, and he forgot to close the garage door. Things like that."

Mrs. Hurley pressed on. "Does he knock all of y'all around like that?"

"No, just my mother," I assured her.

"Don't it make her mad? Don't she never do nothing back?" Mrs. Hurley took a loud quaff from her coffee cup.

I licked some syrup from the corners of my mouth. "Well, sometimes she says 'if you do that again, I'm going to kill you.'" I took another bite of the biscuit.

"Aha! Good for her!" She cheered my mother on. "Then what does your daddy do?"

"Well, sometimes he just says 'so what.' And sometimes he just gets in his car and goes to Tampa to see his girlfriend." The big eyes grew still wider and even more crossed. I saw that I had scored.

"Mother of God! What's *her* name?"

"Eunice," I said. Eunice was my current favorite name. "I can't say her last name. It's hard to say. It's Spanish or German, I think. Something like Rigoletto," I added, borrowing from my father's Red Seal record collection." I finished my biscuit and gulped down the coffee, pleased with my story and the effect it was having on Mrs. Hurley.

"Well, no wonder! Now here's your aspirins. They's Bayers. Best money can buy. Tell your mama she ain't got to return them, poor thing. And when you go home, you tell your daddy he better pray to God to forgive him."

I shook my head. "He doesn't believe in God." To her stricken face, I quickly added, "But he says Jesus Christ almost every day."

"Well, see! There you are!" she said. "He wouldn't get away with that in my church!" She pressed the pills into my hand and hurried me through the house to the front door as though I were tainting the breathing space along the way. There was a figurine of Jesus impaled on a cross on the living room wall. He was holding his own bleeding heart in delicate, effeminate hands, and he wore a thorny crown on his bowed head. I could smell Octagon soap rising from the linoleum floor as she rushed me to the door and down the front steps.

I skipped down the driveway, and when I reached the gate, I looked back. She was still standing, fat and rigid, in front of her house, her eyeglasses flashing signals of outrage in the sunlight. I waved and thanked her for the biscuit. On the road toward my house, I met Mr. Hurley in his truck, and I stepped out of the ruts to let him pass. He waved and drove on. I knew his wife would regale him with my story, and I was satisfied that I had provided her with something savory.

By the time I reached the church, all the mourners were gone, and the church door was locked. My mother and father would be home. I saw my brother taking his cowpony to the stable, and I begged to ride the pony, but he refused because the little horse was too tired and hungry. Then I nagged him to let me ride home on his back. He refused that too. He was in a bad mood. Everyone was depressed about Bird Dog, except the Hurleys, who figured Bird Dog got what was coming to him.

My mother and father were sitting on the front porch. My father was reading. My sister was inside doing her homework. My brother sat down on the steps next to Balder, who was stretched out on the floor. No one spoke.

At last my mother asked me, "Where were you all afternoon?" I told her I had been to visit the Hurleys. Then I remembered the aspirin tablets still clutched in my hand.

"Mrs. Hurley sent you these. They're for your sick headache."

My mother looked up, surprised. "Why does she think I have a sick headache?"

"I don't know," I said. "Anyway, what is a sick headache?"

Osiria and Horus

Slim and vertical as a sapling, the black woman was moving toward us fast. Her eyes were fixed straight ahead, and her stride was long and fluid. She balanced a large washtub of folded laundry on her head. A ragged child trotted along at her heels carrying a heavy stick. Both woman and boy were barefoot and silent.

"Who are they?" I asked Lutie Bea after they passed us on the dirt road. We were on the way to Lutie's house, which was set back in the woods about two miles behind my house and the school. I didn't go home to play with her very often, because she lived with her grandmother, who was demanding and sickly and sat in a rocking chair and smelled of Vick's Salve.

"Them's powmetter niggers. Don't never mess with them. I wisht we ain't seen them." Lutie Bea rolled her eyes around and shook her head.

"Why? Why not? What's wrong with them?" I was eager to know, because I had never seen these black people. In fact, I didn't know that any black people lived in the backwoods in Sweetgum Slough.

"Them's bad folks," Lutie warned. "They'll pull your hair out and hang it on a tree. Then they'll do a spell on you and cause you to kill your mother." She rolled her eyes again and nodded, tucking straight brown hair behind one of her ears.

"Why do they do that?" I asked.

"They can't help theirselves. Black folks is like that. All of them. You got to be careful. They can put a spell on you right when they walk by you, and you won't even know it. I wisht we ain't come up on them." We both glanced behind us, but the woman and boy were out of sight.

I studied Lutie Bea, and I saw that she looked especially sweet and odd. As we walked on, her words buzzed around in my head, and I thought of my mother's mother, a Southern Baptist lady from South Carolina, who told my sister and me that we must never say the word *nigger*. She said that black people should be called *darkie* or *colored*. She said that only *white trash* called them *niggers*. And I wondered why my grandmother thought that *darkie* and *colored* were more acceptable terms, but I took her word for it. At six years old, I didn't want to be *white trash*. I looked again at Lutie Bea walking satisfied and happy beside me, and I saw her in a hard new light. It felt mean and unfamiliar to me.

"Where do they live?" I asked.

"Who? Thems? They live way over yonder in the powmetters and scrubs," she said, pointing. "They don't come out of there much. Just sometimes. The mama carries washing to Brooksville. She takes in washing for somebody over yonder. She walks so fast she can get there and back with her youngun before sundown. Niggers can walk faster than people."

"Why doesn't the little boy come to school?" I asked Lutie Bea, who was my only source of knowledge and wisdom at that moment.

"To school?" she screeched and put her hand over her mouth and laughed. Lutie had a goofy laugh. "'Cause niggers can't come to our school. It's against the Lord," she said, employing both jurisprudence and divinity to good effect. "They don't go to no school nowhere. Even if they did, it wouldn't do them no good. They can't learn nothin' nohow 'cause they heads is solid bone." She gave me a long, close look to see how that would go down.

"How do you know that?" I asked, being careful not to discourage any other forthcoming remarkable information she might offer. I was rewarded.

"Meemaw told me. Meemaw said her granddaddy oncet seen a dead nigger in the war, and they weren't nothin' in his head but solid bone." We had arrived in the shade of her cool, swept yard. The old woman she called Meemaw sat in a rocking chair on the porch, shelling peas. Lutie and I sat on the steps at her feet, resting from our long, hot walk from school. There was no detectable affection between Meemaw and her granddaughter, but each had a function in the life of the other. Meemaw gave the child a place to live after her mother died and her father went to prison. In return, the old crippled woman had Lutie to fetch and carry for her. They seemed satisfied enough with the arrangement.

Meemaw was the descendant of early Anglian settlers, and therefore she was local blue blood. Her forebears had come to Sweetgum Slough so long ago she didn't know their history. She said that they had come down to Florida in a wagon from somewhere in the hills to the north. People like Meemaw were scattered throughout the woods around Sweetgum and had retained much of their Appalachian culture. There was a bond among them which newcomers and drifters, like the DuLacs, did not share.

When Meemaw's only son was sent to prison for making illegal whiskey and she was left to raise Lutie Bea, the community quietly came to their aid.

Someone took syrup to them at cane-grinding time. In the fall, when hogs were butchered, people gave them meat, and men came by with their plows and mules and prepared the soil for a small garden. Someone else gave them seeds from last year's crops. Little Lutie Bea learned to plant and weed under her grandmother's supervision. But Meemaw grew to expect and demand favors, and when they were not promptly forthcoming, she sent Lutie to ask for them. Still, even in those hard times, her neighbors were patient and giving.

Meemaw looked up from her peas. "You younguns can go git you a biscuit. They's some back yonder in the kitchen if the ants ain't got to them." It was the first time she had spoken since we arrived from school.

Lutie Bea and I went into the dark, old house. It smelled of medicinal eucalyptus, like Meemaw, but it was clean and bare, and the biscuits tasted good with plenty of cane syrup on them.

After we ate the biscuits, we had to do some chores. Most of the country children were required to do chores when they arrived home from school, and I joined in when I went home with them. They taught me to do things that I would never learn from my mother, who I would most likely find working through an algebra problem, watching birds, searching for some elusive thing, or writing a story.

On that day, Lutie had to wash some heavy pots, and I swept the kitchen floor. We both cleaned lampshades, and I held the metal funnel while she filled the lamps with fresh coal oil. We shelled some corncobs and fed the hard kernels to the chickens in the backyard. Then we went back out on the front porch with Meemaw, who had finished shelling and snapping peas.

"I wisht I had me some good salt hog to cook with these here field peas," she said. "You younguns walk on down the road to Crawleys and ast them if they can spare me a little chunk of salt pork."

So we took another long walk through the pine stands, palmettos, and oak knolls, which stretched as far as we could see on either side of the little dirt road. Buzzards circled and drifted overhead in their lofty quest for death on the ground, and the stillness was only interrupted by tiny gnats milling around our eyes and noses. By the time we got the salt pork and returned to Lutie Bea's house, we had only enough time to climb one large, spreading live oak.

We never tired of climbing those splendid trees, even though the bark was rough and concealed small scorpions that stung us painfully until we learned how to spot them, and the Spanish moss draping the limbs housed billions of chiggers—minute arachnids that burrowed into our flesh, causing red welts and fiery itching.

The live oak limbs were long and graceful and dipped low to the ground. We could straddle the lower ones and ride them like wild ponies. We could hang upside down from others, hair falling toward the ground while we watched a giddy world of leaves and blue sky above us. And sometimes we fell as we tried to leap from one limb to another, and we hit the ground so hard that we couldn't speak or cry for moments until our breath returned and filled us with life and the terrible need to try again.

The sun was getting low, and I had to start home if I were going to get there before sundown. I loved the walk through that wooded acreage behind our property. It was wild and uninhabited for miles, and there were no fences. Cattle grazed freely and rested in the shade of the live oaks. There was a grassy rain ditch beside the rutted road, and during the rainy season, it filled with amber water. Little gray fish appeared on the surface from nowhere, and sometimes I would see a strange iridescent minnow among them flashing its tiny bright scales in the sunlight.

I stopped to look into the water beside the road. Watching wildlife was soothing and it taught me patience and the profound pleasure of being still. I waited without moving, and soon they came to the surface. They swam about in a swarm, nipping at each other and trying to ferret out some miniscule food particle. Although I didn't have my Mason jar and dip net with me, I watched the minnows, poised above them like a predator. More and more arrived to join the others in their endless quest for food. In those long days of the Great Depression, sometimes it seemed like every living thing on earth was hungry and searching for something to eat.

Then I heard it. A heavy step, a snort, and the crunch of grass being cropped and chewed. I looked up and felt the cold pain of fright run from my stomach through my limbs. Autry! The white bull was grazing his way toward me, followed by several bony scrub cows of his current harem. He hadn't seen me. I crawled behind a low bush and crouched down, but Autry was sure to discover me as he came closer, so I knew that I had to find a better solution.

Frantic, I looked around for a tree to climb, but I was in a clearing. There were no oaks anywhere near and only one pine sapling a short distance away. I knew that I could shimmy up the young tree if I could get to it before Autry got to me. I ran as fast as I could, not daring to look back to see if the big bull were charging. Breathing hard, I scrambled up the little tree, pulling with both hands and pushing with my knees and feet until I reached the top. Then I looked around for the bull.

Autry stared up at me, chewing the last bite of his grass. He tossed his great head, swiveled his eyeballs and snorted. He looked at his ladies to make sure they were safe from me, but they had lost interest and had begun to graze again. Then he took a few steps in my direction, stopped, stretched his thick neck, and emitted a few short screeches. I closed my eyes. When I looked at Autry again, he had lowered his head and was pawing up the earth and slinging it over the hump on his back.

I climbed higher. And that was a mistake. My little sapling began to bend downward. I slid lower a few notches, but it didn't help. Small as I was, my weight was too much for the slender young pine. Down we went together. I found myself hanging by my hands and feet as the tree bent lower and lower toward the ground. I closed my eyes and began to scream and howl.

"Wha's de mattah wit you?" I looked up into the black face bending over me and into eyes as blue and shining as little bubbles. "You sho can make some racket fo' sich a little baby. I gotcha. Now leggo de tree." I released the sapling, and it snapped back up almost as straight as it had been. I felt a firm grip under my arms as she lifted me away from the tree.

Still screaming, I cried, "Where's Autry?"

"Who Autry?" the tall black woman asked as she stood beside me.

"The bull," I sobbed, as I clung to her, my arms encircling her legs. She picked me up with her strong black arms. She had a sweet, wild scent about her which I found comforting, but I had a death-grip on her neck anyway, as she carried me back to the road.

"He gone. Horus ain't gwine let him git you. He gone, baby. See? He way out yonder. He gone. Horus done run he off." Her voice was as soft as moss. I continued to cling to her as she carried me. I saw the boy running and hollering behind Autry, his stick raised high.

"Git out! Git!" he yelled, jumping over clumps of palmettos as he ran on his skinny legs, little strings of black licorice. I watched in terrified amazement as the huge white animal trotted away, grumbling as he ran, his dewlap swinging from right to left under his chin, his ladies following.

With Autry in retreat, the boy came to look at me, still holding the magic stick he had used to defeat Goliath. He had a little round face with huge black eyes and a mouth full of big white teeth. He wanted to know my name, but I still couldn't speak. He smiled at me, and his mother put me down so she could look at me. Again, I was startled by the opal eyes in her dark face. It occurred to me that she might be blind like my grandfather, who sat in his leather chair reading Braille and seeing nothing with his dead, white-blue eyes. But her eyes were full of life, and at that moment, I thought that everything beautiful and good in the world had settled in those two light spots on either side of her soft, flat nose.

"Whey yo' Mama at?" she asked, wiping tears from my face with her long fingers. I pointed in the direction of my house, still silent. "Wha's yo name, baby? Ain't you got no name?" I hesitated. Then she said, "I be Osiria.

And he be Horus. He be my boy." I told her my name, and she smiled for the first time. "Don't holler no mo'. We gwine carry you to yo Mama."

Osiria picked me up again. I knew that she thought I was younger than six years old, because I was so small. I indulged her. I felt safe and happy riding on her bony hip and enjoying the sweet earthy scent of her skin and the comfortable rhythm of her long, steady stride. Horus followed us, and we reached my back gate well before sundown. She deposited me there on top of the gate post, the way she would restore a fledgling bird to its nest. Then she turned without a word and walked away, followed by the boy. When Horus looked back at me, I waved. He smiled again and brandished the stick he had used to drive Autry away into the palmettos.

I perched on the gatepost and watched them float away from me on the narrow road, never changing their pace. And finally they were not there. They were gone. The way a dream ends without definition. From one moment to the next.

First Prize

"Where's that little box at?" Belle's hands were on her hips, her face thrust forward, close to the blank features of Arla Frady.

"What little box?" Arla stared back at Belle with Orphan Annie eyes.

"That little box you stood on when you kissed Bartow's ass," Belle replied. There were shrieks of laughter from the younger schoolchildren, who had gathered around the two girls in a corner of the early morning schoolyard. Belle's collection of tangled, coarse curls quivered on her sassy head. I cowered behind Dorcus and Nina Tatum. From that safe haven I welcomed Belle's return from the silent grief she had been nurturing since her brother, Bird Dog, was killed by his horse.

All the girls had been twittering about Bartow Bailey, the new star of the neighborhood. He had come to live with his Uncle George, whose frame house was within sight of the school. A good-looking, blond boy of sixteen, he rode his uncle's horse to the mailboxes in front of the school and pretended to read his mail while the girls giggled and ogled him and the boys viewed him with a mixture of envy and suspicion. He was too old to attend our school and old enough to quit school entirely if he wanted to. And that is what he did. It added to his mystique and made him a hero to the children in Sweetgum Slough. But Belle honored no heroes.

I moved still farther away from Arla and Belle, pulling gentle Nina with me. Her sister, the more aggressive Dorcus, confronted Belle.

"You shut up, Belle. Arla ain't done nothin' to you. You let her be or I'm gonna bust that big mouth of your'n." Nina broke away from me and ran to get their older brother, Floyd. Just then, I heard a gurgle behind me. Wilene Stitchfield stood there gawking at the two girls, her orange eyes glittering in her red face. Some spittle collected in the corners of her mouth.

"They goin' to fight." Wilene looked gleeful, and she waved her good arm around in an erratic gesture and tried to jump up and down, but her deformed body could only writhe in response to her efforts.

"Shut up, Slewfoot!" Little Cooter Crawley gave Wilene a contemptuous shove, exercising his right to abuse her because she was crippled. "Red-headed sapsucker. You ain't got no sense." Cooter threw a stick at her. It hit Wilene's cheek and just missed her eye. She cried out and reeled backward, holding her face with her good hand and falling hard on her shriveled side.

Nina arrived with Floyd, who first grabbed Cooter by the back of his neck and then gave him a sharp kick on his behind.

"What you think you doin', little Banty shit? Git out of here." Cooter ran to the school porch, crying and holding his rear end. "Now, who else wants a kick?" Floyd stood there looking at the group of agitated children, and we stared back at him. He was tall and thin, and I saw that he looked almost exactly like his mother, who was short and fat. While I tried to come to terms with that finding, Belle stepped forward and confronted Floyd.

"I don't want no kick, Floyd. I just want to know what Arla done with that there little box." Belle smirked at the boy, cocking her head with its pile of wild hair.

"What box you talkin' about?" Floyd asked, swallowing the bait.

"The one she stood on when she kissed Bartow's ass!" Belle mocked him in a comic voice, and the children snickered and pushed each other in glee and stared at Floyd to see what he would do next.

"You got a dirty Boggs mouth, Belle. You ort to git your mouth pumped out with coal oil. Now git away from Arla and leave her be. She ain't done nothin' to you, did she?"

"Oh," Belle said, still mocking him. "She ain't done nothin' to me 'sides bein' a chickenshit stink beetle. I ain't scared of you, Floyd Tatum." She strutted up to the boy, opened her considerable mouth wide and stuck out her tongue. "Look in here. Take a good look at my dirty Boggs mouth. Want to see my dirty Boggs booty, too?" Belle was about to pull down her underpants when someone shouted.

"Teacher's coming. Here comes Miz Cockshot!" We scattered like biddies under the shadow of a hawk. I ran with Nina up on the porch. Belle, undaunted, swaggered to the well to get a drink of water. Arla waited at the gate for Mrs. Cockshot, who had just parked her little car under the oak tree in the churchyard across the hardroad.

Frowning, Mrs. Cockshot said, "Now what bad news you got for me today, Arla? You always got something. I can't even get in the schoolhouse without you worrying me with something another. So what is it today?" Mrs. Cockshot carried books and papers, and a worn leather purse hung from one of her big arms. We couldn't hear Arla, but we knew she was telling the teacher about Belle. Mrs. Cockshot walked to the well where Belle was drinking water and watching over the rim of the gourd dipper.

"Belle, are you talking nasty out here?" The teacher was irritated about being assailed so early in the morning.

"I just ast her a question," Belle answered, slowly pouring water from the dipper back into the well.

"So what was it she ast you, Arla?" Arla stared straight ahead without answering or blinking, her eyes like two blue holes in the sky. "If you can't tell me what it was Belle ast you, don't take up my time." And Mrs. Cockshot stomped off to the door of the school, unlocked it and went inside muttering and slamming the door behind her.

Belle shifted her smoky eyes to Arla. "Now ain't that too bad. Teacher don't like no tattletale goat turd neither." The rest of us stood looking at the slammed door. We knew that Mrs. Cockshot wouldn't ring her bell for a while, so we began whispering among ourselves.

Like two cats at the end of an unresolved fight, the girls took cautious leave of each other. Arla slunk out to the girls' privy, looking back over her shoulder now and then to make sure Belle was not following her. Belle began to swing around on the structure covering the well. I joined her there because I wanted to know more about Bartow Bailey and the little box.

Belle laughed, "You so dumb, Biddy. They ain't no box. I just like to git Arla mad 'cause she thinks she's the queen of the world."

Mrs. Cockshot put us through our morning routine. After the Bible reading and the Lord's Prayer, she let us sing every Stephen Foster song we knew, including "Old Black Joe," my favorite. At seven years old, I didn't know whose gentle voices were calling old Joe or where he was agreeing to go, but I sang with passion and in what Mrs. Cockshot and Stephen Foster believed to be Negro dialect. Singing had a calming effect on us.

The teacher wanted to work with the seventh and eighth grades all morning, so she told the rest of us we could draw and color. That was an additional reward. I ran over to Belle's desk, and we decided to draw a picture together. Our crayons were old and broken, but we found a large piece of paper, and sitting side by side at Belle's desk, we began to talk as we drew.

"I'll make the trees and houses, and you make the people," Belle said. "You make good people." We drew and colored for a while without speaking. Then Belle said, "I seen a pitcher-show oncet. They was a elephant in it. He was something. I never seen such a thing before." Belle studied her drawing.

"I saw real elephants in a parade in Sarasota," I said—truthfully, for a change. "And camels and zebras, too." I often adorned my facts with more splendid details, or I invented my stories from beginning to end. But Belle never questioned my integrity, and she accepted my fantasies for whatever they were. We colored with deep concentration, stopping at intervals to study our creation.

Then Belle asked, "Did you ever wisht you had something nobody else got, Biddy?"

I thought about it. "No. I don't think so. Like what?" I stopped drawing and gave Belle my full attention.

"I wisht I had me a little, itty-bitty live elephant. About this little." She put her crayon down and held her hands five or six inches apart. "And I'd be the onliest person in the world that had one. And I'd bring him to school and keep him on my dest and he'd hand me my pencils with his long nose thing." We laughed and began coloring again.

"Mrs. Cockshot won't like it," I said, already envious of Belle's little elephant.

"Oh, she won't care. Miz Cockshot don't bother me none. My little elephant will just lie down real good and behave hisself," Belle said.

"What about when he has to go to the privy!" I asked, presenting another obstacle to this adorable elephant.

Belle was thoughtful as she colored in some flowers. "He can do it in my inkwell," she answered. I ain't got no ink in there nohow." Then she added, "And I'll put some moss in my dest under the inkwell so he don't mess on my books. Then he can pee all he wants to and his itty-bitty turds will be so little it won't make no difference where he does 'em." We laughed hard, and I almost slid off my end of the seat. Mrs. Cockshot walked by to see if we were drawing nasty pictures. She frowned at us in warning and went back to the older children.

"Can I play with him sometime?" I colored in a leg of my woman, whose head reached the eaves of Belle's house. The leg was quite a bit larger than her other leg, but it was very shapely.

"Uh-huh," Belle answered in her most indulgent voice. "I'll let you and Wilene play with him. 'Cause you so little and dumb, and Wilene throws fits. But not shitnose Arla Frady."

"I'm not dumb," I said, unperturbed.

"No, Biddy, you ain't dumb like you can't do numbers and read and such like. You just don't know nothin' worth knowin'."

"Like what don't I know?" I didn't feel defiant so much as surprised and interested. I knew that Belle was my friend.

"You don't know pea-turkey." Belle laughed and reintroduced the little elephant to the conversation. "You can play with him all you want to. But you can get you a little critter, too."

"Where do I get it?" I asked.

"Same place I got mine. They's aplenty of 'em." Belle opened her dark eyes wide as though viewing a stampede of animals on the veld.

"Oh. Then I'm going to get a little zebra for my desk." I borrowed her green crayon to finish my woman's other leg. I'm going to name my zebra Eunice. What's your elephant's name?"

Belle thought. "Elephants ain't got to have no names. Just people. Mine ain't got no name." The morning passed fast, and we finished our picture and made two more before Mrs. Cockshot rang the noontime recess bell.

I ate lunch at home with my mother and father, and then I hurried back to school to join my friends in the shade of the school porch. They had forgotten the early morning ruckus, and they were laughing and eating when I arrived from my house. None of them lived near enough to go home for lunch, so they brought their noonday meal in shiny metal syrup buckets with lids and thin metal handles. We called our midday meal "dinner." In fact, we had never heard the word "lunch," and we called our evening meal "supper." The people in Sweetgum Slough ate three hot meals a day if they could find enough food.

I was curious about my friends' dinner buckets. I went from one to the other to examine their food. The six Tatum children always brought the same thing. Their syrup cans contained cornbread and lima beans cooked with salt pork. The boys got an extra large portion of beans and sometimes a biscuit in addition to the cornbread. The two Stitchfields ate together because no one would eat with Wilene except her older brother. Each had a sweet potato in its skin and a piece of cornbread.

Delano had the best dinner, and he liked to share it with me even though I had just eaten at home. He would let me choose between his sausage biscuit and a big square of delicious, soggy syrup bread. Mrs. Whatley often included an extra square of syrup bread for me. Sometimes Delano had a hardboiled egg, a slice of salty ham, cornbread, and some collard greens. He would offer me the egg while he ate every scrap of the rest.

The three Dulac girls had the most exotic buckets. Depending upon the success and extent of Claude Dulac's foraging the night before, the girls brought fried frog legs or fish, stewed turtle, squares of cold grits, alligator chunks, squirrel legs, biscuits, or cornbread. And they liked for me to sit with them while they ate and have some of their food, so I did that whenever I had room left in my stomach.

In those years, most people in Sweetgum Slough had to scrounge for food, but every child had something in his bucket. Even the Greshams, a poor struggling family who lived on the dirt road leading to the scrub, always saved something from supper the night before. Even if it was only turnip greens with whole, boiled turnips. I was afraid to share the Greshams' food, because they were sickly children.

Mrs. Cockshot ate lunch inside at her desk and was often joined there by Mr. Whatley, who tethered his horse to a fence post by the mailboxes. Mr. Whatley came to the school on the pretext of getting his mail from his box under the oak tree. But his visits to the school had become more regular since his daughter, Ruby, graduated and went, with my sister, to the high school in Dade City. Sometimes Mrs. Cockshot left the schoolroom for long quiet talks with him on the porch. Then the older children gave each other knowing looks and made comments under their breath. Or they made signs with their hands and fingers and laughed when Mrs. Cockshot turned her back. Delano looked sad and lost his gaiety when his grandfather arrived at school on his horse.

The Whatley-Cockshot romance didn't interest me as much as it did Belle, who was obsessed by what she called "doing it." My passion was for games, which I played outside with my friends. I was undersized and physically untalented, but I ached for the freedom and exuberance of recess, when we would run out the door and choose teams or continue some game we had begun before school in the morning.

We played Red Light, Red Rover, and Crack the Whip. I was not considered a team asset, but when I finally heard the captain call my name, my heart leapt, and I ran as fast as I could to join the chosen. These were wild and thrilling games that resulted in several broken limbs, but we were allowed to continue playing. Mrs. Cockshot never supervised our games or interfered with them. If we were injured, she treated us with Mercurochrome and iodine, or she sent us home.

London Bridge was an ancient singing game that required no skill. It was a girls' game, but once in a while, a small boy joined us, and the older boys made fun of him. When we finished singing, and everyone had been chosen, a tug-of-war followed. And because we were of all ages and sizes, we were often bruised when we ended up in piles on the ground with our small arms stretched beyond their sockets.

Hail Over was the best game, because it involved the whole school population. Two of the older boys chose the rest of us for their teams. It was exciting to be chosen and devastating not to be chosen. In the beginning years, I was often not chosen for this game because I was small, even for my young age, and I was clumsy and babyish compared to the country children. I cried like an infant when I was hurt, but I also cried when I wasn't chosen, so team captains had to determine which route to take with me. Ultimately, I was allowed to join the game to some degree. Sometimes they made me sit on the school steps to eavesdrop on the other team. That was cheating, of course. But I would accept any role. It was better to be a participating criminal than a rejected crybaby.

The two teams stood with our leaders on either side of the little school building. The shingled roof was steep and as slanted as a child's drawing, and we all looked up there in anticipation as the leader on the other side yelled "Hail over" in a loud, drawn out, almost musical voice. Then a baseball-sized rubber ball came bouncing and rolling down on our side of the roof. We all rushed to catch it before it hit the ground. If someone succeeded, we became very quiet and ran around to the other side to try to hit as many people as we could with the ball before they could escape to our side of the building where they would be safe. Each time the ball hit its mark, any of us could pick it up and throw it at another person on the opposing team. I usually ran around and watched my teammates hit people with the ball.

Then it was our turn to call "Hail over" and throw the ball over the roof and wait to see if the other team was coming around the building to get us. Most of the older boys could aim the tough rubber ball well enough to hit just our legs. But the country boys were strong and threw hard, and sometimes they hit our heads and faces. That was painful and caused tears and welts, but we played on.

The best game of all happened unexpectedly one early spring day, and for once, I was the winner. A large mother hog with a new litter of eight or nine piglets bumbled into the schoolyard through the open gate. She was a razorback rooter, one of many feral hogs in the area, and used to providing for herself and her young. She was also fierce and well-armed for protecting her tiny new babies. When we came out of school at the end of the day, we spotted her rooting in the rich soil under the oak tree, her black-and-white babies milling around their mother. She grunted to her young as she located gritty earthworms, acorns, and grubs for them. They squealed and pushed each other and shoved their little snouts into the black earth, imitating their mother to perfection.

One of the older boys closed the gate and several of them began chasing the little pigs. When one pig was caught, squealing and struggling, the ferocious old sow charged the captor. Soon the whole school was chasing piglets, and a game evolved. If we were agile enough and fast enough to catch a pig, we ran with it and passed it on to someone who could run faster before the infuriated sow ripped into our legs with her sharp tusks. Pigs were passed from child to child amid shrieks, squeals, and the terrifying roar of the mother hog, who twisted and turned in a desperate effort to save her litter.

Pass the Pig was a dangerous game, and I was too afraid to join in. I crept toward the gate, and just as I opened it to escape the scene, Sonny Mosley rushed toward me holding a pig straight out in front of him. Both of their mouths were wide open and the sow was at Sonny's heels. Before I could stop him, he pushed the squealing pig toward me, and I took it from him. I managed to slip out of the gate and close it before the sow reached me. I stood outside the gate with the hysterical piglet, and the sow ran off in pursuit of another kidnapper.

Someone was standing by my side. I looked up at Bartow Bailey, who was watching the game and holding the reins of his horse while it grazed at the boy's feet. "Well, I guess you got you a pig," he said.

"Is it my pig?" I asked, instantly falling in love with both the pig and Bartow.

"It is now," he answered, still watching the wild activity in the schoolyard. The sow and her young had commandeered the attention that he believed to be his due. He determined to wait until someone noticed his arrival.

Holding the pig and staring at Bartow, I thought of Belle and Arla and the little box. I tried to imagine Arla with her creamy hair and uninhabited face standing on the little box kissing Bartow's behind. But before the image had completely formed, the pig quivered in my arms, and I realized that it had stopped squealing. I looked at the young animal. Exhausted, it stretched its short neck over the crook of my arm and closed its eyes. I saw that it had long, white eyelashes. It also had black dirt in its mouth and on its tiny hooves and clinging to its soft, round belly.

"Look! It's quiet," I told Bartow, who wasn't interested. "Look at my pig, Bartow. It's gone to sleep. I'm going to name her Eunice." Bartow ignored me and moved closer to the gate to give the world a better view of himself.

I walked away holding my prize in my arms. No one saw me leave.

Malaria

When my mother finally came down with chills and fever, we found ourselves at the mercy of our neighbors. Among themselves, they organized a system of rotating home health care. Their concern for us came from their hearts, but it was prompted by my mother's many contributions to the sickbeds of Sweetgum Slough.

Our predicament became known in the community after Enzo Hendry arrived early one morning and found us all groaning in our beds. Later, when he went to collect our mail, he met Ole Stitch in front of the school and told him that we were all down with the bad fever. Our news spread from there.

Malaria was working its way through Sweetgum Slough, and with my mother's collapse, our whole family was in some stage of the disease. My father was in relapse. He had gotten up too soon to help my mother nurse the rest of us. But his fever returned, and he had to go back to bed on a day cot in my brother's room. My brother was up and down. He continued to feed his pony and the other animals, but the fever brought him back to bed in the afternoon. His care of the animals slowed his recovery and kept him restless.

My very bones ached, and I had strange deliria with gnarled dreams and wild visions. I was hot and cold at once, and the sheets hurt my skin as I tossed and struggled in bed beside my feverish sister. She consoled me as well as she was able, but the large capsule of quinine from the old doctor lodged in my throat and gagged me. I cried for my mother, but she was too ill to respond. We were a sorry lot.

Mrs. Tatum came first and hustled around our house, sweeping and cleaning like a tractor and cooking food that smelled of collard greens and some outrageous item from her barnyard. When a stray whiff found its way from the kitchen to his bedroom, my ungrateful father murmured something to Jesus and turned his face to the wall. He was not a Southerner. It took either a Southerner or a carrion gourmand to eat collard and turnip greens or to be attracted by their aromas.

My sister and I could eat nothing most of the time. When our fever retreated a bit, Mrs. Tatum coaxed us to sip some pot liquor from the collard concoction. It tasted good, and it restored a little strength to our limp bodies.

I could hear my mother sighing in the next room, and I whimpered to be with her. She had nursed us all as long as she could—shaking thermometers, bathing our faces and arms with cool washcloths, feeding us soft-boiled eggs, milk toast, and chicken broth, and reading to us. But then she, too, began to chill and shake.

Mrs. Tatum did her best for us, but she had to go home to her eight children after a few days. She was replaced by Mrs. Boggs, Belle's mother, who arrived under an alarming coat of cosmetic material—heavy powder and rouge and bright red lipstick. When he saw her, my father closed his eyes and alerted Jesus again. He did it so softly, it sounded almost like an expression of controlled admiration. It was not.

Mrs. Boggs cackled and commented to us with her greasy red lips as she stomped around our house, examining everything from our silverware to my father's treasured records. I knew Mrs. Boggs only in the context of her own home, when I went there to play with Belle after school. She was a slovenly woman and always a little drunk, surrounded by her wild sons and grown daughters, Hetty and Burma. Hetty was married to Buck and they lived there, too, with their three vacant-looking little boys, who came to school every morning with their aunt Belle.

Burma was young and shifty-eyed. She had a head full of curly black hair and large soft lips over white teeth next to smooth tan cheeks. She was a skinny girl, but her breasts were large and pendulous and moved around suspiciously under her dress, like she was hiding a couple of ferrets there. People in Sweetgum Slough said that Burma was *ruined*. She didn't look ruined to me. And I liked Burma. She made a delicious sweet confection that she called divinally, and she gave it to Belle and me to eat after school. I liked all of the Boggs, even though they shared a peculiar family odor and a wanton, careless manner as they lived all together in that little shack.

Sometimes, Belle and I had to walk a long back road to Frank Frady's house to get moonshine for Mrs. Boggs. When there was no money for it, we had to go anyway, and Belle had to beg and promise to pay later. Begging and promising were not among Belle's natural approaches, and she hated to do it—especially in front of her archenemy, Arla Frady, who stood beside her father, watching Belle's struggle with her big, blue doll eyes. But Belle had a fierce and protective loyalty to her family and a tender spot in her heart for her mother.

When we had the whiskey in tow and were out of their gate, Belle would turn to me and say, "Shitface, pissing moonshiners. They ain't nobody—making stinking stumpwater." And we would hurry to get the moonshine to her mother.

Mrs. Boggs took her turn in our infirmary, and we were too sick to resist. She refused a comfortable cot on our enclosed back porch. Instead, she made a pallet for herself on the open front porch where a reluctant Balder took one look at this arrangement and moved his sleeping venue to the far corner of the porch behind the rocking chairs. Noble responsibility would not permit him to completely relinquish his summer sentry post to this dubious bedfellow.

In fact, as she well knew, the front porch provided Mrs. Boggs with easy access to various male members of the community who came prowling around at night like feral tomcats in the shadows of the pine trees, causing Balder attack after attack of righteous outrage. After a night of moonshine-enhanced activity among the palmettos, she would be found the next morning asleep on her pallet, her makeup so smeared, we could hardly recognize her features. She looked like roadkill, but she would get up, unable to cackle, and head for the kitchen where she made strong coffee for herself and, incidentally, for my father, who was the only one of us brave enough to drink the boiled brew.

Later in the day, the whole house smelled of fish. Mrs. Boggs ordered her sons to bring a string of catfish every afternoon, and she filled my mother's heavy skillets with lard. Then she deep-fried the fish until they twisted in the pan. She served them to us whole with a huge mound of grits, and she poured the fish grease over everything as a finishing touch.

When my father saw it he said, "Jesus in Hell!" He liked fish the way my mother prepared it, but he ate grits reluctantly and only with sugar and cream, like a foreigner or a Yankee—certainly not with fish.

Little Ducie Stitchfield came next. She was shy and would not look at us. Barefoot and silent as a puff of smoke, she went to the kitchen, her poke bonnet clutching her little fat head like a guardian owl, and began cutting okra that she had brought from her garden. Then she went to the backyard, took a Plymouth Rock hen from her croaker sack, wrung its neck, and plucked it, carefully putting all the feathers back into the sack. I sat in the kitchen in my pajamas, weak as I was, watching her cut the chicken into serving-size pieces.

In answer to my questions, she either nodded her poke bonnet or she said something that sounded like "y'arm" or, what I gathered was its negative counterpart, "n'arm." I gave up on her without too much delay and went back to my bed, where I could watch the clouds outside my window.

When she brought the food to us, it was tasty and digestible. And with new appetite, my sister and I ate her sweet potatoes, stewed chicken with okra, biscuits, and butter. When we thanked her, she said "y'arm," nodded her bonnet, washed the dishes, fed the cat, and then went out to the shed and the stable to take care of the chickens, the cow, and the pony.

We all slept well. The next morning, Ducie arrived at dawn with a steaming bucket of milk that she had just extracted from our midget cow, and with the milk she made a glorious pot full of oatmeal porridge. We ate it with genuine pleasure and a little bit of cane syrup. Then, Ducie gave us a firm nod of her poke bonnet and left without a word. I followed her to our front porch, and as I watched her walk barefoot down our lane, I saw her spit a man-sized projectile of dark brown tobacco juice in a perfect arch over the palmettos.

A procession of women found their way into our house after Ducie left. Most of them were hearty people who wanted to help us and did. But we all rejoiced when Sadie Whatley left her many duties in the Whatley household and took over our management until we were healed. I was overjoyed because Sadie and I were on hugging terms. She was Delano's eighteen-year-old sister and surrogate mother, and I knew her well because Delano was my best friend and I spent long, happy hours in his home among his big family.

Sadie was a buxom, round-hipped girl with deep cleavage she couldn't conceal if she tried. And she didn't try. Like all of her family, Sadie was healthy and handsome. Her cheeks glowed, her white teeth were even and well-set in her mouth, and her blond hair was finger-waved according to the rules of the day. The Whatleys made up for their peculiar humor by the good fortune of their fine Celtic features, their industry and warmth, and their easy laughter—even if it took several puzzling minutes to realize that nothing was funny when they laughed. And they were full of laughter.

We were all relieved when Sadie marched into our Malaria-ridden household and took charge. She called us all, including my parents, by the variety of nicknames we used for each other. Some of these names were hard to take, even when spoken by close family members, and some were intended to be insulting and were downright outrageous or reserved for times when we were angry with each other. But Sadie latched on to them, and no one had the heart to object. It's hard to lash out at someone who is bathing your feet or changing your sheets or bringing you a delicious meal, although my brother looked miserable when she called him "Cookie" and my father winced at "Daddylonglegs."

I thought it was very funny when she called us by our nicknames, and I told her so. She laughed long and loud and said, "Me another." All the

Whatleys said "me another" when they wanted you to know that they shared your feelings.

But we took Sadie in stride. My mother ignored her seeming impertinence in favor of her good nature, generosity, and capabilities. My father enjoyed the cleavage and rolling round hips as she moved about our house, bringing us good food from the Whatley farm and cooking it with expertise in our kitchen. She stayed until our mother was strong enough to take over from her, and by then, we were all feeling well—at least for the better part of each day. But malaria was a stalker and hovered around, waiting to strike again. We knew that we had to be patient and careful.

Old Doctor Thistlethwait came out and made his rounds through the country and stopped at our house in his black Ford sedan. The epidemic had been hard on him, and he looked weary. He took our temperatures, looked down our throats, listened to our hearts, tapped our knees, and thumped our backs. He asked for a drink of water and swallowed a quinine capsule himself. Then my father and I walked with him to his car. He opened the back door and took out a large brown paper bag full of glass jars of all sizes.

"Do me a favor, friend," he said to my father, handing him the bag. "Throw this old pee away for me. Everybody gives me a jar of pee when I leave. They think I need to see their pee. They can't pay me, but by God, they always have a bottle of pee for me. Just get rid of it. I don't care what you do with it. Put it on your mantelpiece, if you want to." He got in his car and frowned down at me from the open window of his Ford. "And don't you tell nobody."

Doctors scared me—even those in my mother's family—but I told myself, as I smiled and reassured him, that I would tell anyone I pleased.

My father stood there holding the bag of urine specimens, and we watched the doctor drive down the lane toward our front gate. We watched him open the gate, drive through, and close it. As he passed along the hardroad beyond our grove of young orange trees, we waved one more time.

"Why doesn't he want to look at the pee-pee?" I asked my father, using our family term.

"For the same reason nobody wants to look at pee-pee," he answered. "Would you want to look at it, for Christ's sake?"

"Not usually," I answered. "But I want to look at this pee-pee," I said.

"Then feast your eyes." He lowered the paper bag and opened it so I could see the jars inside.

"How do people get it in those little jars?" I asked my all-knowing father.

"It takes imagination and probably some acrobatics," he answered, closing the bag. "And now I think I will just dig a hole and bury it, if you don't mind."

I had more questions, but my father was not in the mood, and we moved on to the shed where he kept his tools and implements. He began to dig a hole behind the shed, and when it was deep enough, he put the whole bag in it. He replaced the soil on top and tamped it down with his brogans.

"There," he said. "May it rest in piss!"

"That was silly, Daddy," I said, laughing.

"I know. I just thought it fit the occasion."

He put the shovel back in the shed, and we walked toward our house. We passed my brother, who had a new spring in his step as he went to feed his pony. In the kitchen, my mother had resumed her most recent premalaria passion. She was making light bread and rolls. The heady scent of yeast and baking filled the house, and I could hear my sister singing "The Object of My Affection" as she set the table in the breakfast nook.

She was in love again. Probably with Bartow Bailey. Everybody was in love with Bartow Bailey. Including me ... and Bartow.

We sat down at our table in the kitchen. It had been a long time since we had gathered together. We studied each other and saw that our faces were pale and our bodies gaunt. But we were healthy again. And there were no strangers in our house, no unfamiliar food, no quinine capsules or thermometers, no aches and pains, no hallucinations or soaking sweats.

I looked around the table at my family. "Guess what Dr. Thistlethwait made Daddy and me do."

Joe Louis!

When he was twenty years old, my father joined the Navy and World War I. He was assigned to a mighty battleship and letters from him to his parents were frothy with youth and excitement. He went to England and France, and in Le Havre, he stood at attention with his shipmates when Marechal Joffre came aboard. He sent his mother a picture postcard of the event with an arrow drawn in ink to Joffre and another arrow pointed to himself.

He did something else, too. He became the heavyweight boxing champion of the U.S.S. Pennsylvania. But he did not write home about that. His mother was still trying to come to terms with the fact that he had a small tattoo engraved on the instep of his right foot.

Throughout his teenage years, my father played a variety of sports, but the one he wanted most was denied him. His mother put her foot down and refused to let him box. She said that it was a ruffian's sport and she would have none of it. But when he got away from her and the Navy assigned him to the Pennsylvania, he immediately joined the ship's boxing team.

Even after he "grew up," he continued to follow the sport—as certain otherwise intelligent, sensitive men will do. He always seemed to know who the boxing stars were, when and where they were fighting and who their target would be for the evening.

And that is why we piled into our car with Balder one hot night in Sweetgum Slough and drove to San Antonio where there was electricity. My father knew where we could hear a radio broadcast of the re-match between the African American boxer, Joe Louis, and his counterpart in Nazi Germany, Max Schmeling.

This was no ordinary world championship match. Adolf Hitler was out to prove the superiority of the Aryan race. He had anointed Max Schmeling to help do the job for him by beating a black man—not just any black man but an American black man at that! President Roosevelt responded with a personal endorsement of Joe Louis, and boxing entered the political arena. The world was on the cusp of a second world war, and nerves were taut.

My mother disliked boxing, but she went with us because she never wanted to miss anything. We children went because we were always ready to go anywhere, and Balder went because he believed that it was his duty to protect us at all times, regardless of whatever foolishness we were up to.

We stopped at the filling station near the little town square and parked our car among a scattering of Model T Fords and mule-drawn wagons filled with sleeping children and tired farm women. Several saddle horses, stamping their feet and swishing their tails at nocturnal insects, were tethered at the edge of the woods, and cicadas began to scratch out their monotonous signals from the pine trees.

A radio blared from inside the small frame building. One electric light bulb hanging from a rafter shone on some men and boys who had gathered around the door to hear the fight. They leaned against the walls or sat on a cement platform that supported the gasoline pumps. Others sprawled in their overalls on the grass around the station, rolling cigarettes and smoking and chewing tobacco. They spoke together in the halting, soft cadence of the Florida flatwoods.

There was a quiet excitement in the warm night air as we all waited for the fight to begin. Balder's big black head protruded as usual from one of the backseat windows while he worked the crowd with his eyes, nose and ears. Nothing escaped his attention, and he produced an expletive warning to anyone who dared come near our car. I sat in the front seat with my mother and father and studied the country people as more cars, wagons and horses arrived and people tried to find places to sit or stand near the door. My brother got out of our car and sat on a fender and my sister stretched out on the back seat.

Peering into the shadows at the side of the station, I noticed that a little cluster of people huddled there. I could not see them well because they tried to keep themselves out of view. But I could tell that they were black people who lived in shanties and shacks in rural parts of the county… the silent, black people who had walked miles through the woods and the humid night to hear about one of their own. As my eyes grew accustomed to the darkness there, I could see the intermittent flash of white teeth or hear the brief wail of an infant.

Suddenly, a ragged young boy broke loose from the secluded group and ran out into the dim light to retrieve a scrap of paper discarded by one of the white farmers. The waifish child snatched it from the ground and ran back on stringy black legs to the darkness beside the filling station.

The farmer laughed and said, "Them little pick-a-ninnies is just like goats. They'll eat anything—paper wrappers, anything. Just like goats!"

His companions laughed and one aimed a stream of tobacco spittle over his shoulder and agreed. "Ain't that the truth!" he said.

The blaring radio became louder as the fight began, but I was still thinking about the little black boy. He was Horus, who had saved me from Autry! Horus, with the sweet smile. And I thought of his blue-eyed mother, Osiria, and her voice as soft as moss. My throat tightened, but I said nothing.

My father got out and stood beside the car to hear the urgent, rapid-fire voice from Yankee Stadium. But before I could release my thoughts of Horus and begin to listen, the fight was over. Joe Louis knocked the German out in less than three minutes. There was no applause. Not a human sound. My father got back into the car beaming. "By God, he did it!"

Men were standing around silenced… staring at the ground and each other, while the obsessive rasping of cicadas underscored the awkward interval. Shaking his head, my father said, "Look at those poor confused bastards. They're glad the Nazi went down, but they just can't cheer for the black man!"

Wagons and mules creaked off into the night. Little cars started to pull away. I looked into the darkness around the filling station hoping to get another glimpse of Horus. The black people were still crouched against the wall in a fearful quiet, waiting for the white men to leave. They knew that their victory had put them in danger. When the last Model T cranked up and drove away, the little group moved furtively out of the shadows toward a dirt road and disappeared into the trees.

The June night held its breath. Then somewhere from the depths of the woods, we heard a clarion call. A single, joy-filled voice ripped through the foliage like a startled bird. It lifted high above the cicadas' lusty chorus, tore through the past and the present and burst into the starlit sky with its clear, sweet message to the world.

"Joe Louis!" it sang. "Joe Louis!"

Godiva

Enchanted, I watched Godiva spread peanut butter over the back of her left hand. She slapped it on in great, thick swathes, like someone making a sandwich for a hungry child. Her fierce old eyes searched the length of the dining table. Then she spotted a bowl of blackberry jam.

"That's the thing," she muttered. I gave my great-grandmother an encouraging smile as she applied a rich layer of jam to her peanut butter. Then, I held my breath as I waited for her next move.

"Godiva!" My father leapt to his feet. All the conversations at the table stopped. I tried to conceal my disappointment while my mother hurried to the kitchen and came back with a basin of water and a towel. Rosebud, my grandmother, came to her mother's side and began clucking and washing the sticky mixture from Godiva's hand.

"You're ruining my sandwich," Godiva said. She looked distressed and angry.

"I'll have to make you another sandwich," Rosebud said, still clucking and fussing.

"You ruin everything I do. They ought to get rid of you." Godiva gave Rosebud a look of purest contempt.

"Hold still, Mama, and let me dry your hand." Rosebud rubbed her mother's old hand with the towel.

"You think you're the Great Mogul." Godiva hurled the insult at her daughter.

I looked at my father, amused. It was funny to think of little, round Rosebud as the Great Mogul. But my father looked sad and serious. He loved these two old women, who were mother and daughter. He had given them pet names when he was their little boy and the star of their lives—their only son and grandson. Rosebud went to the kitchen with the basin, and my father sat down beside Godiva. He kissed her cheek and held the scrubbed hand.

"Where are we?" she demanded. My father looked out of the dining room window.

"We're about to come into the station. When the train stops, you can stretch your legs," he told her. He looked at me and smiled. He knew that I understood Godiva's demented obsessions—including her perpetual "train trip." He also knew that I enjoyed participating in her fantasies.

The family meal was over. Godiva glared at her plate, which now contained neatly cut rectangles of bread covered with peanut butter and jam. My mother and Rosebud cleared the table with my sister's help. She was quick and efficient, slipping around them and stacking dishes on the kitchen tables. I admired my beautiful and capable sister and longed to be like her.

My father cranked his Victrola and placed a Red Seal record of Benjamino Gigli's silver voice on the spinning disc. Then he stretched out on the living room rug, hands clasped under his head, and closed his eyes. My brother and Pap wandered off to inspect the young orange groves.

When we visited my grandparents, Pap and Rosebud, in their gulfside town, my sister usually took charge of Godiva after the midday meal. I would skip down to the bay, lie on the warm dock, and watch fiddler crabs sweep the sand in waves of crackling blankets until they dropped out of sight into their holes. Or I would creep farther out on the dock where green needlefish floated like wary sticks on the surface of the deeper water and striped sheepshead pecked at oysters clinging to the pilings below.

This time, my grandparents were visiting us in our home in the country. I swelled with pride when Rosebud asked me to take Godiva outside for a walk.

Godiva, like all of my father's family, spoke with a northern accent that I thought made her sound harsh and commanding. She carried her tall, slim body as straight as a fence post. It was difficult to find a trace of her renowned earlier beauty under the hard latticework of her face. My father said to look long and carefully, and the girl in the riding habit with the heart-shaped face would come as alive as her photograph on his desk.

But now she walked ahead of me, taking such long strides that I had to trot and jump to keep up with her, and sometimes I bumped into the back of her legs.

"We should have brought your leash, Taffy," she said, frowning down at me. "Then you wouldn't be such a nuisance. Walk smarter or I'll have to put the choker on you and take you back to the coach."

My father had said that we should all join the adventure of her delusions. In that light, I accepted my role as Taffy, although I felt it was demeaning. Taffy had been Godiva's least favorite Cocker Spaniel—a rogue animal, untrainable, stupid, and the subject of unflattering family accounts of ridiculous behavior. She had been an idiotic, legendary dog. For the sake of the game, I tried to do as she asked, but Godiva took charge of the outing. She headed for the stable where my brother kept his horse. I was beginning to wonder if I were up to this responsibility.

Godiva had been an accomplished equestrienne when she was green-eyed Sally Hyatt and before she married her young physician. They settled down to a privileged Victorian life in their small Midwestern town, and they had a long, undisturbed marriage. After my great-grandfather's death, Godiva came to Florida to live with Rosebud and Pap. She had never been close to her only child, and she disapproved of her son-in-law because he left a promising business to venture into Florida orange groves. She found great solace in her grandson, my father. But when he married my mother and left home for good, her last light dimmed, and she gradually faded into a world of her own design. She boarded a train in her dissolving mind and began a never-ending journey north to the little town of her youth.

As we approached the stable, my brother's chestnut horse raised his head from the grass, blew from his nostrils, and walked toward us, his ears pointed forward with interest. I hoped Godiva wouldn't open the gate, but she lifted the latch and swiveled inside with the horse before I could stop her. I was afraid of the animal unless my brother was with me. It had bitten me twice and kicked me, but Godiva seemed to have a way with it. She closed her eyes and let the horse cradle his head in her arms.

"Oh, you smell so good." She stroked his head and his quivering nose.

"His name's Tony, Godiva," I said, wondering how anyone could think Tony smelled good. I didn't like the odor of horses.

"No, it's not. You don't know what you're talking about. You say anything that comes into your head. His name is Riley. Go in the stable and get his hat, so I can ride him." She stroked his face and jaws, and she lifted his lips to see his teeth.

I ran to the stable, climbed over the half-door and looked around in a panic. I knew that I must keep her from riding the horse. I saw Tony's bridle hanging on a hook, and I quickly opened the top of his feed barrel and threw the bridle in it, hiding it from view. Godiva appeared in the doorway with Tony's head over her shoulder.

"I can't find it, Godiva," I said. "He doesn't have one."

"One what?" she asked.

"A hat," I said.

"Of course not, you damn silly little fool. Now get down from there and let's go." Godiva had taken to swearing because it embarrassed Rosebud, who was a church woman. Relieved, I followed her out of the stable yard on the path leading to the pond. Again, I had to hop along behind her, because the path was narrow. Although I had successfully steered her away from the horse, Godiva was still in charge of the moment. When we came to the edge of the pond, she bent down from her waist and touched the clear water. She put her wet fingers in her mouth.

"That's good enough to drink. I'm going to take a bath."

"No, Godiva," I begged her. "You'll get your clothes wet. And maybe you'll catch a cold."

"Catch what?" she hollered, as though she couldn't hear me.

"A cold," I repeated.

"It's not cold. This water is warm as tea," she responded in her hoarse voice.

"I'll tell you what. Let's lift up our skirts and wade in it," I said.

I helped her remove her Red Cross shoes. She steadied herself by grasping the top of my head as I knelt down to unlace her shoes. To my dismay, I saw that she wore thick cotton stockings. I tried to remove them, but I soon found out they continued on up to some mysterious place beyond her knees. I began to tug. Something snapped up there under her skirt, and one stocking fell and nestled around her ankle. I quickly pulled the other one down and slipped them both over her toes and off. I stuffed them inside her shoes. Then I removed my sandals and tucked the hem of my skirt into the legs of my underpants. Taking her hand, I led her into the shallow water.

Her old bony feet looked white and brittle as she shuffled along over the soft grass bottom of the pond. Immediately, little minnows came to peck at our ankles and toes. Godiva leaned over to study them. I put my hand in the water to let them nibble my fingertips.

"Don't bother them," she said. "They want to know what we are. They have a right to that." I gave that some thought and decided it made more sense than most of the things she had said to me so far.

"Let's go a little deeper, Godiva." I led her into the pond until the water touched the hem of her dress.

Standing there in the warm water with the old woman developed into an intense and happy moment. I lifted her hand against my cheek. And when I looked up, I saw that her eyes were closed and she was smiling. With both of my hands, I examined the old claw as though it were part of something else. Like a discarded glove or a crumpled paper. I turned it from palm to back where her diamond rings sparkled through a film of peanut butter.

I looked down into the water. Our bare legs seemed to wobble as the surface of the water moved. Then I looked closer. At first, I thought I saw narrow, black, slimy leaves. Then I realized that they were attached to our legs. I screamed and began dragging Godiva toward the grassy shore. First, I pulled the leeches from my legs and hurled them away. I had never touched a leech, although I had seen my brother remove them from Tony's hooves. Godiva watched in annoyance while I cleared her legs. The whole operation took less than a minute.

"Why are you jumping around like that? I knew I should have brought that choker. This is the last time I take you out, Taffy." Godiva found a sunny spot away from the water and sat down on the grass like a girl. Still shuddering, I brought her shoes and stockings and dropped down beside her. I released my full skirt from my underpants and spread it out in a circle on the grass around me. It was my favorite garment, because it was covered with small flowers and large brilliant butterflies. I had worn it for my grandparents' visit.

Godiva leaned over me. A strand of white hair escaped from the combs and chignon at the nape of her neck and hung over my lap as she examined my skirt.

"They are perfectly beautiful," she said. I stood up and held both sides of my skirt out to give her the fullest view of the butterflies. She gasped and locked her knotty fingers in front of her. "Oh, my. But what do you feed them?" She looked at me, her eyes watering from sunlight and pleasure and wonderment.

I dropped down and rolled over in a backward somersault, out of control with mirth.

"Leeches." I told her between laughing spasms. "I feed them leeches."

The spirit of the moment caught on. She threw her head back in the sunlight and laughed out loud with me, exposing all of her own sturdy yellow teeth. A strand of hair fell across her open mouth. I did a forward somersault and found myself sitting beside her again. All of a sudden, she leaned down and looked into my face as though she were seeing me for the first time. The lines and angles were gone. Her green eyes were soft and bright. And for a ripple of a moment, I saw the girl with the heart-shaped face.

"Oh, you are a sweet, fair little thing," she whispered. I tried to hold her there with my eyes to keep the moment safe. She straightened up, legs and bare feet stretched out in front of her. Her expression changed, and she took on a dark look. "But you weren't the one I wanted. I wanted the other one. The one with fur as shiny as a copper penny. She never gives me what I really want."

"Godiva, I'll put your shoes on. We have to get back to the depot. Your train is getting ready to leave." I felt sad as I slipped her shoes onto her feet. I would not attempt to replace her stockings, so I put them into a large pocket in her dress. I tied her shoes and pulled her to a standing position. This time, I walked in front, and Godiva followed me up the path toward our house.

When we arrived, I could tell that everyone had worried about us, but no one scolded me. Rosebud clucked and flapped over Godiva's bare legs. Godiva was silent. Pap kissed my mother and shook hands with my father. My father kissed and held Godiva. Rosebud kissed me and told me that I had to visit her soon. My sister kissed Rosebud and Pap, and Rosebud settled Godiva into the back seat of the big Nash. Then Rosebud got in the front seat, and Pap lit his pipe and took his place behind the steering wheel while we all stood around the car.

As they drove away, I saw Godiva through the side window. She stared straight ahead, as rigid as a profile on a coin. Or the way train passengers looked when you saw them passing through little Florida towns on their way back north to some other life beyond the palmettos, the warm rain showers, and the moan of a bullbat just before nightfall.

The Slough

Fishing was a living word, filled with powerful scent and bright image. It was a state of mind, a mystery to be solved, a missing part to be found. If caviar-filled sturgeons had been waiting for our bait in all those little, dark lily pad-covered ponds and shallow tannic creeks, we could not have felt greater excitement when we went fishing. Something wild and rare would come out of the stars to take the hook at the end of our lines. It was a dream we could play over and over again, even when the dream turned into a traumatized little bluegill or an ugly, inedible gar. Fishing was a way of nurturing hope and keeping imagination alive.

My father did not fish, so he was never part of our fishing parties. My sister sometimes joined us, but she would become dreamy and distracted, propping her pole against a tree with the line hanging limp in the water while she wandered into the woods to study the trees or the shadows on the ground, and at home later, she would produce an astonishing painting or charcoal drawing or a poem. Or she would put her pole on the ground and slip into the fishing hole to swim and wash her red hair in the soft water.

My mother, brother, and I were the fishermen. One or two of us, or all three, fished almost every day. Fish were fickle. And we developed theories about their biting habits. My mother thought that it was not a matter of habit. She believed that fish biting or not biting was established by her own hunch as to time and place. My brother was just as convinced that fish bit best before a rainstorm, after a rainstorm, early in the morning, and just before sunset. That philosophy served him well, because it provided him with a wide expanse of fishing opportunities. As a result, if we followed him and his blueprint, we could get caught in a storm and a torrential downpour. I liked my mother's romantic hunches better, so we often fished together. I would come home from school and find her tying the bamboo poles to our car, and away we would go.

My brother was the most talented fisherman among us—and the most productive. Anyone who wanted to catch fish went with him. He had a great love for the prairie lands that extended for miles behind our property, and he would fish the big lakes there alone, wading through them and casting for bass with his rod and reel, often returning home after dark and always with a good catch. Before my father gave him a horse, he walked to the distant prairie lakes to fish, and one time, as he was coming back at dusk, he was stalked by a hungry panther.

The animal was probably attracted by the smell of the fish hanging from my brother's belt, or perhaps, by the scent of the thirteen-year-old boy, himself. He glimpsed the large cat from time to time as it moved low-bellied through the trees and underbrush near him, snarling and growling in the shadows.

Terrified, my brother was tempted to run, but he knew better. He took a shortcut to our back acreage and felt a little safer when he finally climbed over our gate where he was enclosed by our fences. But he knew that fences were no obstacle to a hungry panther, so he moved on as fast as he dared.

When he heard Balder's powerful bark, he knew that the panther would turn back. In the shelter of our kitchen, we saw that he was white and shaken and that tears stained his face. He was just a stripling boy, but he was as brave as any man. Only a few years later, my brother received a presidential citation for heroism at sea. As he stood in the kitchen and told us about the stalking panther, we listened with serious faces. The next day, my father bought a horse for my brother and a .22 rifle for protection on his trips to the prairie lakes.

Reports of panthers were rare. Cattlemen camping out in the prairie ranges were more afraid of razorbacks, the vicious, wild mongrel hogs whose ancestors were said to have been brought by Spanish explorers. Panthers were spotted over the years; calves and pigs were killed and devoured now and then; but there were no attacks on people. Still, I slept close to my sister that night, and for days after my brother's fright, I made Balder go with me everywhere I went.

We had several good fishing locations. My favorite place was within easy walking distance. To get there, we followed the hardroad, our connection to everywhere. If we walked for a short hour, we came to the slough bridge, a long, crude wooden structure that shuddered and rattled when my father drove over it in our car. The bridge spanned a watery area of shallow streams and deep fishing holes and little islands with narrow, sandy beaches where wading birds poked around for snails and frogs and turtles dug nests in the sand every spring and laid their round white eggs to warm in the sun. Sweetgum trees grew in the surrounding hammock, and great cypress trees soaked their swollen trunks in the shallows, while their polished knees stood at attention around them, guarding them, posted there like little brown soldiers.

My cork wobbled up and down, and when it went under the amber water and stayed there, I held my breath and watched it make deep, wild turns. I tried to lift my line, but it was taut and heavy. With all the strength of my few years, at last I was able to pull the fish onto the sand, where I stood barefoot under the bridge. I watched the big perch gasp and flap around on the wet sand. My brother said it was the biggest warmouth he had ever seen. I was wild with pride.

The two of us had been fishing at the slough all afternoon, and together, we caught about ten fish—a combination of perch and bream that country people in Sweetgum Slough called stumpknockers, yellow-bellies, bluegills, and warmouths—or anything else that occurred to them and seemed to fit. My big perch was about twelve inches long and by far the giant of our catch. I could hardly wait to get home to show it to my parents and feel the glow of their praise. I knew that after my brother scaled and cleaned our fish, my mother would season them with salt and pepper, dredge them in cornmeal and fry them to a delicate brown. We loved to eat their fine-grained, sweet flesh, complemented by coarse grits with butter, hushpuppies, sliced tomatoes, spring onions, and cucumbers.

My brother knelt down and showed me how to remove my fish from the hook. Then he added it to our string of fish and replaced the entire catch in the water, fastening the string to a stake that he had driven into the sand. Squatting there beside him, I watched my big perch as it twisted around in the water, flashing its fat yellow belly and gulping water while it struggled among its captive kin. I hated the sight of the desperate animal, and I hoped that it would soon join the other fish on the string in a comatose acceptance of its fate.

I baited my hook again. We were using small, gray crawfish that we had caught by dragging a dip net along the bottom of a shallow ditch near the slough. The crawfish looked like miniature lobsters, and I didn't like to push the hook through their brittle thorax while their little fan-like tails beat a frantic plea against my offending thumb and forefinger. But I was learning, and impaling the unhappy crustaceans on my hook was part of the process.

Holding the baited line in one hand, I took my bamboo pole in the other and followed my brother along a narrow strip of sand to another part of the slough. He decided that we had time to try for one more fish. We came to a deep hole where the water was almost covered with lily pads and their pale yellow blossoms. My brother motioned for me to stop and fish there, and he moved on.

He had switched over to his rod and reel to cast for bass. The slough was not known for bass, but my brother liked to try a new lure he had carved and painted himself or to cast and practice his skills.

I stood on the sloping bank, still holding the pole and baited line in my two hands as I watched my brother disappear around a bend in the slough. A great blue heron, disturbed by our arrival, rose up from a mud flat with his long legs dangling beneath him like a gigantic mosquito. I could see his ferocious yellow eye and his hoarse, klaxon alarm bruised the silence of the slough. Lesser wading birds scurried to safety among the lily pads, and two busy didappers ducked under the water, leaving only a pair of identical circles to show where they had been.

A basking cooter slid off a log and slipped into the water, making an almost inaudible, liquid sound. Moments later, I heard a faint gasp, and I saw his head, pointed and shining, among the water lilies where he had come up for air and to take a look at me.

The cypress trees moaned as a brief and unexpected breeze ruffled their fine, green foliage and stroked their limbs. Rising to the surface of the subtle sounds around me, holding my breath and my fishing pole, I stood silenced by the voices of the slough. But the intermittent wheezing of my brother's reel when he cast out, and the *plop-plop* of the lure as he reeled in, disrupted my reverie, and I moved on.

The water was deep, so I pushed my cork higher on the line before I dropped the crawfish into a clear spot among the lily pads. A few curious mosquito minnows gathered around the cork until they lost interest and swam away. I stood still, my eyes on the cork. Dragonflies twitched above the water, and to my delight, one of them perched on my cork, gripping it for a moment with tiny, cloying feet before it rose into the air, sunlight glancing off of its slender, mica wings. Dragonflies came to the slough to dip their abdomens in the dark water and deposit eggs there before they flew away to die.

Changes of season were announced only by innuendo in Sweetgum Slough. Sometimes I didn't know what time of year it was, but it must have been spring, because the cypress trees were pale green, water lilies were everywhere, and tiny black tadpoles wriggled at the water's edge. The eternal sun seared the watery landscape of the slough, and turkey buzzards lounged around on updrafts of air, making elegant circles high in the clear sky. The hot sun and the vultures were forever fixed above us. They were there, like breathing or heartbeat.

I shifted my weight, moving as little as possible. My cork remained still. I began to wonder if I had put the cork too high on the line. I thought that my bait could be on the bottom or even nibbled away by small fish, and I would be wasting my time. But I resisted the urge to take my line out of the water.

Instead, I watched the heron stalk over to a small sandy island in the middle of the slough. He leaned over and struck a pose as rigid and gray as driftwood, his head cocked and his evil, yellow eye frozen on something in the water. Then he unleashed his long, powerful neck and brought up an eel, impaled on his dagger beak. The surprised snake-like fish escaped the weapon, fell onto the sand and made a frenzied effort to get back into the water. The heron lost all composure and engaged in a graceless and ridiculous dance, as he stabbed holes in the sand over and over while his mercurial prey dodged and wriggled.

Just when it seemed that the eel would outwit the heron and reach the safe haven of the water, a large hawk dropped out of the sky, sank her talons in the eel, and flew away with the prize. It was so fast, the heron didn't see it happen. He looked frantic and foolish and puzzled, all at once, as he searched the sand and the shallow water's edge. Finally he gave up or forgot, pulled his head down into ruffled feathers, hunched his shoulders, and took a depressed nap on the little island.

Herons had several names in Sweetgum Slough, but local people called them squawks for their loud, coarse cry. More often than not, the gangly bird ended up on a supper table if nothing more succulent could be bagged that day. In those years, a generous array of things became edible to the creative mind and empty stomach.

The scene and its drama had been so absorbing I forgot about my cork. I still held my fishing pole, and when I looked, I saw that the cork had not moved. I took my line out of the water and found the little dead crawfish hanging in one piece on the hook. Not even a nibble.

My brother arrived with no bass to show for his efforts and said that it was time to start home. I wound my line around the pole, stuck the hook into the cork, and tossed the limp crawfish corpse back into the water where it immediately attracted a gaggle of curious minnows as it sank to the bottom.

I followed my brother back toward the slough bridge. The air was a little cooler as the sun turned pale orange behind the cypress trees, and the sky began to prepare itself for the late afternoon show. We soon reached the bridge and the sandy beach where I had caught the big warmouth. I ran ahead of my brother to the stake that anchored our string of fish. I dropped to my knees beside the stake. It was still firm in the ground. Then I saw that our fish were gone. The string had been severed, and part of it lay on the sand. My brother came running when he heard my shriek, and he knelt beside me to examine the theft while I continued to howl.

"Stop that! Stop crying. You're scaring everything in the slough," he said.

"I don't care. Somebody stole my big warmouth," I sobbed.

"Somebody stole all of our fish, and I know who did it," he said. He was crawling around on his hands and knees. "Look at these tracks."

I stopped crying and studied the sand through my tears while my brother examined the piece of cord still tied to the stake.

"What are they?" I asked, staring at the dozens of small animal tracks around the stake.

"Coons," he said. "Coons. Probably more than one, too. And look at this cord. It wasn't cut with a knife. It was chewed."

We followed the tracks as they led to the cypress trees and into the hammock. We could see where the fish had been dragged over the sand and then through the grass. Then I remembered to cry again. I walked back to the stake and sat down on the sand and bawled at the top of my lungs.

My brother poured the remaining crawfish back into the ditch. He told me to carry the empty bait bucket. I cried louder. Finally he said that he would leave me at the slough if I didn't stop. He said that we had to go or we couldn't get home before sunset, and I said that I wanted my big perch. And I sat next to the stake and declared that I would not leave without my fish.

"This is what I get for taking a crazy little crybaby fishing," my brother said. He put the bucket and the fishing gear down and came over to the stake where I sat with my head on my knees.

"What's the matter with you? There's nothing we can do. The coons took our fish because they were hungry. And they have babies who are hungry back in the hammock somewhere. They have to feed their babies. They're probably having a big dinner with their babies right now," he said, almost pleading.

"How many babies?" I asked. I stopped crying and focused on the image of the raccoon family banquet with my warmouth as centerpiece.

"Oh, maybe ten or twelve. There could be three or four coon families having a big coon party right now. They never had so many fish in their life. They sure never saw a big perch like yours in their whole life. They must be the happiest coons in the hammock with that big warmouth," he said, sensing that he was making progress with me.

"But I wanted it! I wanted to show it to everybody at home." I said. "And now nobody will believe me because I make things up."

"Well, I'll tell them about your fish, and they will believe me, because I don't make things up," he said. "I'm going to tell them how big it was. And I'm going to tell them how you caught it all by yourself." He hoped I would not cry again.

I stood up. He handed me the empty bait bucket, and we started home. The low sun had disappeared, and the sky was a scarlet smear through a changing screen of cypress trees, oak knolls, and pine stands. I followed my brother, and as I skipped along the hardroad behind him, the flaming sky burnt itself out.

I thought of the raccoon family and my big, stolen warmouth. I thought of the great blue heron and his awkward, demented dance. I wondered if the hawk fed the eel to her babies in a nest somewhere close to the sky. I increased my pace to catch up with my brother as we hurried to get home before dark. The sky turned soft and pink, and the song of the slough faded behind us.

Lost and Found

My mother liked to get up before daybreak. Especially in the early spring when birds were courting and singing and building their nests. She liked to get dressed and walk into the pinewoods and around the pond with her binoculars. Before dawn, she would stand still and listen, and when it grew lighter she studied the trees with her binoculars and surveyed the pond area for wading fowl and waterbirds. Then she would come home and cook eggs and bacon and hot, coarse grits for us before we left for school and Enzo Hendry arrived to work in the young orange groves with my father.

I liked those early hours, too, and sometimes I went with my mother on her bird rounds. I had to be quiet and willing to listen. She would lean down and whisper the names of the birds to me, but once in a while I recognized a bird call on my own.

There was a great variety of birds, and she knew them all. Brown limpkins, twitching their tails and limping along on long olive legs, searched the water's edge for small mollusks and frogs. Sweetgum folk called them "nigger boys" in those days when no one either thought or dared to object, much less protest. And curlews arrived in flocks and probed the mud around the pond with their long, curved bills. They had to be wary, because their fat breasts were delicious and made a favorite breakfast for hunters everywhere in rural Florida.

I loved those bird walks with my mother. She knew birds by sound and sight, and if she wasn't sure about a bird, she searched through her books until she found a likely answer. One early morning like that, I went on to school after breakfast. I liked getting there before anyone else arrived. When I reached our front gate, I saw Claude DuLac's truck approaching on the hardroad. At first, it was barely visible in the morning mist. As it came closer, I could see that it was piled high and listing to the left. Claude's pirogue was secured to the top of the cabin, and it protruded over the hood and over the truck bed. Claude and Odile sat in front, and Vinny stood between them.

I climbed up on the gate, and as the truck sputtered closer, I saw Mut, Lizzie, and Maddy sitting among tubs, pots and pans, and mattresses—almost the way they were when I first met them. But this time, I had known them for a year and a half. The whole family had become my friends, and the girls were my schoolmates. I even recognized the tub where I had bathed Vinny when he was an infant, the oilcloth tablecover where we had eaten Odile's spicy food. I knew, with immediate great sadness, that they were leaving.

As they passed me, I scrambled over the gate and ran behind them in a panic, hoping the girls could see me. I waved with all my might, and I called their names, but they moved on away from me. I ran after the truck calling to them, but the girls sat motionless in the truck bed, their eyes toward wherever they were going while the rude motor of the truck stifled my voice. They would not have expected to see me there at that daybreak hour. Dejected, I watched the truck and its precious cargo disappear in the gray, damp light. I walked on to school and sat alone on the porch, my early morning joy in disarray.

Delano arrived before the others. We sat together for a while, and I told him about the DuLacs.

"It ain't goin' to bother me none," he said. "Them girls uz dumb. They couldn't even talk right. And they ate gopher," he added in disgust.

"They did not," I said. "They ate turtles. Not gophers," I said, defending the dignity of the DuLac palate as well as I could.

"Uh-uh. I seen gopher in their dinner buckets lots of times," Delano said. "I know fried gopher when I see it." He looked at me, his face full of conviction.

"It was turtle every time. I know because I ate it too," I told him.

"Then you ate gopher, too. You ort to wash your mouth out with coal oil, 'cause gopher is nasty. And you better take some salts, too!" he said.

"Well, I know it was turtle. Claude only catches turtles. He never catches gophers. Anyway, what's so bad about gophers?" I asked.

"Don't you know?" Delano looked around to be sure no other children had arrived. "Gophers is like girls. I mean *big* girls like Ruby and Sadie." He was leaning close to me, his huge eyes swimming in their own beauty and guarded by double rows of long black eyelashes.

"Well, they sure don't look like girls," I said. I had seen the big, awkward, prehistoric land tortoise that stumped over the sandy scrub, eating plants as it went and digging burrows in the ground, which it shared with snakes and the occasional rodent.

Delano moved still closer. "I don't mean they look like girls. I mean they do what girls do." He stared at me, and I stared back. Then Delano whispered, "Gophers bleeds."

"Everybody bleeds," I said. "So what."

"No. *Everybody* don't bleed. Just girls bleeds. And girl gophers. Out of here." He stood up and pointed to his behind.

"When do girls and gophers bleed out of there?" I asked with acute interest.

Delano sat down and opened his dinner bucket.

"Soon as they get tits," he told me. "They get tits one day, and they bleed the next—if it ain't Sunday." He took a large syrup cookie out of his bucket. He broke it in two and handed me half.

"But gophers don't have tits," I said.

"I know it," he answered. And we chewed and swallowed for a while.

"Then why do gophers bleed?" I asked.

"I don't know. Maybe they got tits inside their shells where you can't see 'em. But they bleed all right. You want to play jumpboard?"

We stuffed the rest of the cookie halves into our mouths and ran to a corner of the schoolyard where the older boys had set a long, heavy board across a log. It was like a low seesaw, but instead of sitting down, we stood on each end. When one of us jumped, the other was propelled into the air, flying higher and higher with each jump. It was wild and exhilarating until the older boys arrived and took over.

That school day seemed long. I stared at the empty seat in front of me where Lizzie had sat, her round, curly head providing distraction from time to time. No one knew much about the DuLac departure.

"I heard Claude was in trouble," Belle said. "Eulice said he done something bad back where they come from. Claude's wife told Eulice they can't stay nowhere for long. Nobody knows what he done or what they want with him."

Mrs. Cockshot just shook her head when I asked her if she knew where the DuLacs had gone. "Folks like that move around. There's no telling what they're up to. Here today, gone tomorrow." She gave me a twisted little smile and told me to go back to my seat, which was her answer to most questions.

The morning routines felt more burdensome to me than ever. The roll call was hollow without the DuLac sisters' unique responses. I missed hearing Lizzie answer "he-aw" and little Maddy's squeal when her name was called. "I hee-ya," she would say, as if she had waited all her life to advise us of her presence.

The Bible verse, as usual, was illogical and senseless, compelling only in its violence and its lilting and peculiar language. Mrs. Cockshot chose verses that depicted God as a sadistic sociopath who spent his time murdering first-born children and animals, spreading boils and other hateful pestilences around the Egyptian population, destroying villages with hailstones, and covering the earth with devouring locusts. I thought of my gentle, profane, loving, and irreverent father and decided that he would make a much better God. But I was wise enough not to share that thought with Mrs. Cockshot.

After the Bible verse, we had to pledge allegiance to the flag of the United States of America. With our hands over our hearts, we began. When we came to the word "flag," we had to extend our arms straight out toward the stars and stripes like little Hitler-Jugend. But we were instructed to turn the palms of our hands slightly upward, a gesture that may have been meant to distinguish us from the young Nazis.

No one knew what "allegiance" or "indivisible" meant or why we had to chant a statement to a flag. Mrs. Cockshot may have known, but she didn't have enough additional vocabulary to explain the words to us. We didn't care. There was something oddly satisfying about performing a ritual in unison with other children. It made us feel empowered and important. And we learned to think it was a good thing to feel mighty and imperious about the flag.

When the Bible and the pledge were behind us, we ended the morning exercises with several songs. We liked to sing, and the songs Mrs. Cockshot taught us were lusty, lively, and sentimental. We sang "Camptown Races," "Suwannee River" and "Nelly Bly." I puzzled over the words, but I sang them with passion while I wondered what a "dolesome melody" was and who sang one to Nelly Bly. I felt better after we sang, but I still had to get through the rest of the day without knowing about the DuLacs and why they left.

Once school was finally over, I hurried home to find comfort from my mother and father, but no one was home to greet me except Balder, who didn't even bother to get up from his nap. My brother and sister had not returned from high school. Then I remembered that my father and Enzo Hendry planned to work at our hammock place all day. I looked for my mother, but she was nowhere to be found.

Depressed, I took off my shoes and walked slowly out of the house to the large oak tree in the yard where my swing hung still and empty, an irritating reminder of my own deserted self. I gave it a vicious hurl and watched it go for the sky, and I watched it swing back and forth until it stopped. Then I sat on it, held the ropes, and pushed myself back with my bare feet. I leaned back and let the swing carry me forward while my head almost touched the ground behind me.

I opened my eyes and saw my mother sitting in the tree high above me, looking through her binoculars into the pine trees around her. The sight of her there infuriated me. She seemed so detached from my anguish, so unavailable to me as she sat up there in the tree pursuing her own interests. I began to cry and wail at her. I screamed, "Goddamit!" and I hurled the swing into the trunk of the oak tree with such a clatter that Balder scrambled up out of his sleep on the porch and began to bark. I ran around the house and down the path to the stable. I climbed up the wooden gate and sat on the gate post. And sobbed.

After a while, I became aware of my mother standing on the gate beside me. She put her arms around me and felt my forehead first with her hand and then with her lips. I knew she was trying to see if I had a fever. The nearness of her, the touch and scent of her, overwhelmed me, and I turned to her and wept until I was empty. Then she helped me down, and we walked back up the path toward our house.

The first violets were blooming. We picked several violets around the palmettos and along the path. Nothing is more beguiling than a new wild violet, blue as Delft and as sweet and coy as a woodland fairy. Later we would put them in a small crystal vase that we kept for the perfect little flowers.

While we peered around for violets, my mother said, "Just look at all the huckleberry blossoms. We're going to have so many pies." I followed her gaze and saw that the wild huckleberry bushes were covered with small white bonnets, waiting to become berries for us to pick.

We sat in a rocking chair together on our front porch. She rocked, and I sat in her lap, limp from my outburst. I told her about the DuLacs.

"I wonder where they went," she said.

"Belle said that Claude is in trouble. She told me that Eulice said he did something bad back home," I told her.

"Well, Eulice may be wrong. Maybe Claude was just going to one of his fishing holes. Maybe they will be back tonight," she said.

"But he never takes the whole family. And all their things," I said.

"It does look like they left, all right," she agreed. My mother was beginning to see the DuLacs as something missing or lost. I knew that she would not be able to resist a chance to help find them. "We can go look at their house later and see for ourselves if you want to," she said. "Do you?"

When my father came home, the three of us and Balder got in our car and went to the DuLac house in the backwoods. Claude's truck had made crude ruts through the woods, and although our car was heavier, we bumped along without damage. Finally, the gray frame house came into view.

We could all see that it was deserted. I looked for Odile's eclectic collection of chickens, but the yard was still. I ran through the front gate, which Claude had restored, between the two crape myrtle trees. I climbed the steps and ran across the porch. The door was unlocked, and I wandered through the house. All of the rooms were empty. I went to the kitchen where I could detect the faint scent of Odile and her herbs. The old iron stove stood there, along with the crude table Claude had built, but the heavy pots were gone, and the shelves were bare.

I went down the back steps and walked out to the worktable Claude had constructed between two oak trees. I smelled fish and saw a fresh layer of scales there, and I knew that Odile had recently cleaned a catch on the table—their last supper. I touched the scales, and for a moment, I felt reconnected. But it didn't last. I moved on.

The washtub was gone and the clothesline was missing. I examined Odile's little herb garden. Mint was spreading all over the borders, but the other plants had been removed. I knew that Odile would have packed them in a box of dark, wet soil to take with her. She would keep them alive until they settled into some other old house in some distant place. I picked a small bunch of mint and buried my nose in it. I chewed a sprig and filled my whole head with thoughts of Mut and her vanilla-laced tea and of Lizzie and Maddy and the funny baby patois they spoke together. I thought of Odile and her raucous laugh when she ran and played with us, her breasts swinging around and leaking milk, her broad feet bare. Odile, ladling out large servings of turtle stew full of little, yellow egg yolks and Claude holding Vinny, smiling at me and sipping his whiskey. And I knew that they were gone. I would not see them again.

I stood in Odile's empty garden, holding the little bouquet of mint in my hand. My father came around the house.

"Well, what do you think? Have you seen enough?" he asked.

"No. I want to stay here for the rest of my life!" I said.

"Don't worry. You will," he said. His voice was soft. I didn't know what he meant then. Maybe he didn't either. But he was right.

We drove away, Balder's head hanging out of a side window. I knelt on the backseat and looked out of the rear window. I watched the DuLac house for as long as I could see it, and then I climbed into the front seat and sat between my parents, still clutching the mint. It felt good to be there close to them. I was tired, and I hadn't eaten anything since Delano had given me half of his syrup cookie.

I thought about Delano and his big eyes and funny, country antics and his eternal energy. I still had Delano. And I remembered what he had told me on the porch before school. I reviewed it for a while. Then I looked up at my father.

"If gophers don't have tits, why do they bleed?" I asked.

"What?"

Uproar

The news traveled fast. Mr. Whatley left his wife, and Mrs. Cockshot was fired.

Firing Mrs. Cockshot was a complicated task since Mr. Whatley was the self-appointed school board president as well as its only voting member. There was great confusion during a hurried meeting of parents at the school on Friday night and another such rally on Saturday where Mr. Whatley's well-known organizational skills were missed.

By Sunday night, the Sweetgum community, meeting in the church, managed to appoint a new school board, which dismissed Mr. Whatley and fired Mrs. Cockshot. And on Monday morning the irate new board marched around posse-like only to find that Mrs. Cockshot had quietly resigned on Friday afternoon, one week before the close of the school year. Neither Mr. Whatley nor his paramour could be found for comment, and the Sweetgum community concluded in a righteous froth that the pair was holed up in some sin-infested love nest.

My father, who did not usually participate in community affairs, attended two of the meetings, which were peopled largely by Mrs. Whatley's kin, the Dawkins clan. My father kept quiet and listened. He liked Mrs. Cockshot, aside from her attachment to Mr. Whatley—my father considered Mr. Whatley to be a horse's ass.

My mother felt compassion for Mrs. Whatley, but she, too, respected Mrs. Cockshot and supported her efforts in our school. Everyone knew that my mother was a teacher herself, so it wasn't surprising that the new school board asked her to complete the last week of the school year while they tried to find a permanent teacher. When Monday morning came, my mother stood behind Mrs. Cockshot's desk as the shy country children, curious and silent, took their seats. I sat at a double desk with Delano whose normal exuberance had all but drowned in the wake of his grandfather's scandal.

Some older children tried to coach my mother in our routines, but she chose to pass over the morning exercises that had been established by Mrs. Cockshot and the state of Florida.

"I'll be with you this last week and some things will be different," she said. She smiled and pressed on. "I'm going to give you some questions to think about all week, and on Friday I want you to tell me what you thought." She wrote the questions on the blackboard.

(1) What is a bird?

(2) Why do birds sing?

(3) Why is an egg the most wonderful and important thing in the world?

(4) If you could fly, where would you go?

She gave us time to read the questions. There was a ponderous silence.

"When we have talked about these questions on Friday and we really understand them," she said, "we'll know almost everything we need to know." She smiled again and gave us a mathematical problem to solve—all of us, from first grade though eighth grade. She assigned us to small groups where older children could guide younger ones.

At first, it was a slow process. We were not accustomed to talking together in Mrs. Cockshot's school. But my mother moved from group to group, and we gradually relaxed as the whole room hummed. A few of the younger children became silly with their newfound freedom and rolled around on the floor until one of the elder students gave them a gruff reprimand or even a swift physical signal.

Finally each group reported its findings, one by one, to my mother while she worked the problems through on the blackboard for all of us to evaluate. Then she let us have a long recess. To everyone's delight, she went out with us on the playground.

From a distance, I watched my friends swarm around my mother. Younger children dared to hold her hands, and older girls hovered nearby. Boys wrestled with each other, viewing her from the corners of their eyes. They all wore that peculiar Minoan mask that children don when they have fallen in love with the deity who is their teacher.

I watched and longed for the comradeship I had felt with my classmates in the daunting presence of Mrs. Cockshot. I longed to fill my lungs with Stephen Foster, to listen to a juicy Bible verse or even one so senseless my thoughts could wander outside the window or around in my head. My mother had invaded my world. I resented her presence in the very place where i was learning to live without her. I felt helpless and angry, and ashamed of these new feelings about my mother.

When Friday came, marking the end of this endurance test, the dreaded bird discussion took place and proved to be a crowning success for my mother, once she convinced the children that birds were more than something to kill and eat and that there were citadels beyond Dade City. In fact, the exchange of ideas was a noisy, happy event that culminated in a brilliant geography lesson and my mother's permanent inauguration as an angel who had come down from Heaven with her birds and eggs and flights into fantasy. At the end of the day, the whole school escorted her to our front gate, so reluctant were they to part with her. I stayed behind on the school steps and waited until the gold dust settled before I started home.

Then summer vacation began. My brother, sister, and I enjoyed long, lazy hours and did whatever we pleased. My brother fished and played his violin and rode his horse through the prairies; and sometimes he helped my father and Enzo Hendry when they needed him. My sister did the things she did better than anyone else. She drew and painted and wrote long stories and poems and helped my mother and inspired me and thought about her next year in high school. I wore sunsuits and went everywhere without my shoes and caught minnows that died and floated belly-up in Mason jars. And one by one, we visited our grandparents in Dunedin and Sarasota.

We ran errands for Rosebud, our little round Midwestern grandmother in Dunedin, and she taught us housekeeping routines that we didn't learn from our mother. Rosebud sent us to the Christian Endeavor, a vacation Bible school, where we had to copy religious pictures and learn Bible verses by heart. My sister, outraged by this affront to her creative spirit, rebelled after only one summer and declared that she would not go back to the "Christian and Devil." From then on, she was released from that detail of her Dunedin visit.

But I went to the Bible school for several summers before it occurred to me that I could turn right one block from Rosebud's house, lap back and go to the park on the bay instead. Then I could spend my morning fishing with string through the cracks in the dock with an excited gaggle of beautiful little black boys. Or I could just sit on the seawall and watch painted fiddler crabs roll in and out of their holes like Dinky Toys.

My brother had long since solved the problem for himself. In most ways, he was a private, honorable boy, but he was not above a reasonable deception. He hid his rod and reel in a hedge the night before Bible school and went fishing in the bay the next morning during Christian Endeavor time.

Rosebud and Pap probably fretted over my rebellious sister, but they must have found some satisfaction in that at least two of us were receiving religious instruction. Or maybe they were not fooled by my brother and me but only too generous to expose us, for they were gentle and loving people.

In Sarasota, another quiet little Gulf town where my Southern grandparents lived, we played cards into the night with our young aunts and uncles and their friends and fished with them early in the morning. We waded all over Sarasota Bay and picked up scallops and ate them that night at my grandmother's long table on Siesta Key. We swam in the Gulf under millions of milky stars at night and thrilled at the green glow of phosphorous on our shoulders. The next day we would flatten like starfish on the white sand beaches of the key and turn as brown as fried mullet.

When the time came, we returned to our home in the country, loaded with the gifts of summer and leaving behind the electric lights, luxurious bathtubs, and flushing toilets of our relatives in the cities. We returned to each other and our pets, to the dark still nights sitting on our porch filled with our own laughter, and to the freedom and familiarity of our life in Sweetgum Slough. We were fired up by the afterglow of new experiences and top-heavy with ideas and plans for the coming year.

My brother and sister were older and more independent than I was, so they occasionally stayed away longer. I needed to come home to my parents, and that was a special time for me. School had not begun, my schoolmates were still occupied with chores on their parents' farms, and the playful and carefree DuLacs were gone forever. I was alone with my parents.

I took to drawing pages and pages of cartoons, which I called funny papers. I sprawled on the living room rug and produced these sheets almost as fast as a printing press. As I drew, I spoke for each character out loud and with so much volume and expression that my father, when he was napping nearby, begged me to whisper. I wrote everything my characters said inside large balloons with strings leading right to their mouths. Some of my cartoons were romantic and inspired by strips like *Tillie the Toiler*. Others were funny like my favorite, *The Katzenjammer Kids*, and some were moral and wholesome like Skeesix and Nina in *Gasoline Alley*.

I climbed our trees and picked berries in the field behind our house, and my mother made the huckleberry pies she had promised. I taught Maxie, my tomcat, to perform circus tricks. I had picnics all by myself, and I sculpted house interiors in a damp, sandy ditch. I dug out the rooms and then molded miniature furniture with hard-packed sand. Then I invented people to occupy the houses. I made up stories and played all the roles in a variety of voices. One of my tenants was a fat girl, named Findelia, who had a throaty voice and did outrageous, silly things that made me laugh so hard I was unable to produce the voices for my other characters.

September was a hot month, and school was scheduled to start right after Labor Day, in the worst of the heat. There was no news about a replacement for Mrs. Cockshot. I thought about my teacher and the Whatley affair for the first time since June, when school had ended in the midst of their scandal.

The thought of school without Mrs. Cockshot made me quiet and uneasy. Mrs. Cockshot had loomed large in my life until then. I feared and worshipped her at the same time—even when she couldn't answer my questions, or when she disputed my information. I had not forgotten that when I had once spoken of Alaskan Kodiak bears, she corrected me and said that bears in Alaska were called grizzlies. When I persisted, she said that grizzlies were bears and Kodiaks were cameras. Everyone laughed at me, including Mrs. Cockshot, and my father laughed when I told him. But he let me know that he was laughing at Mrs. Cockshot rather than at me.

Even so, she remained a powerful presence in my life. I could not imagine school without her. The short week with my mother as teacher had been unnerving. How would it be with a total stranger? I began to fill up with anxious thoughts, and I developed a neurotic facial tic. When my father noticed it, he said, "For God's sake, get your mind off of school before you develop St. Vitus's dance."

So my mother took me to several poultry expositions where we saw exotic chickens, ducks, geese, peacocks, guinea fowl, and doves. We both loved to ogle the strange and beautiful birds. On one occasion, my mother bought me a diminutive Bantam hen and rooster to add to my collection of pets. Another time, somewhere else, she got me a little setting hen with a wild headdress of white feathers and ankles to match, and a clutch of tiny eggs.

My father and Enzo Hendry built a neat chicken house where my chickens could roost each night and where I could lock them away from nocturnal wildcats and rampaging rodents. They constructed a fence around the area and stretched chicken wire over the top to protect the tiny chicks from hawks and other flying predators during the day.

So I became a poultry farmer while I waited for school to start. I sat for hours in my chicken yard, supervising the incubation of my eggs. After they hatched, I watched my diminutive, puffy mother hens speaking softly to their adorable babies while they scratched around for invisible delicacies and sang Banty songs in the sunshine.

We also went to a livestock fair in Brooksville. My father went with us, even though he wasn't interested in seeing the cows, bulls, mules, and hogs. My father was not interested in farming or any of the accoutrement of a farm. He tolerated Sparkplug, who helped prepare our fields for my father's orange groves. And he was happy to give my brother a cowpony, provided the boy took total charge of the horse. He let me have as many pets as I wanted, but he, himself, was a one-pet man. My father loved Balder. He cooked the dog's food, took him everywhere he went, and didn't sleep at night until he was sure that Balder was comfortable and settled. But my father took us to the fair because it started early in the evening and we would not get home until after dark.

It was a large county fair with bright lights, a merry-go-round, a Ferris wheel, and loud, cranky music. We ate hot dogs, and my father bought me bright pink cotton candy, which spun from a machine over a cardboard cone. We watched the high school marching band led by country girls with big bare thighs who twirled batons and wore white boots with tassels and pranced like sturdy ponies.

I rode a wild-eyed carousel horse while I ate the huge ball of cotton candy. When the music stopped, I threw up over the wooden steed's head and neck and I fled before anyone could connect me with the spectacle. Still clutching the empty cardboard cone, I glanced back once and saw that the horse's mane was somewhat pink and one eye was partially obscured, giving him a milder, kinder look.

I searched for my parents, but they had wandered off somewhere. The band marched on to the football field where the girls with big thighs tossed their batons into the air and caught them—or not. A crowd gathered at the edge of the field under the flood lights, and I decided to join them, although the activities of the marching band were static and boring. In the shadows back from the field, there were some green wooden benches where older spectators could sit away from the glaring lights and watch the parade.

As I passed by, I saw a couple sitting on a bench under an oak tree. Through the shadows, I recognized Mr. Whatley and Mrs. Cockshot. I caught my breath and moved closer. I stood behind another tree so I could study them without being seen. The light from the football field cast a pale glow over the old lovers. I saw that they were not sitting close together the way they had on the school porch when we peeked around the door to spy on them. They were not touching each other. She sat stout with her legs crossed at the ankles and her big arms folded over the old leather purse in her lap. Her face was hard and broad like it always was. But her dyed black hair had faded to white at the crown, and it hung, untended, to her shoulders. She watched the marching band as though it were a funeral procession.

Mr. Whatley sat on the bench, one leg crossed away from her over the other. I recognized his boots and the ten gallon hat he had always worn on his head in his days of grandeur, sitting proud on his fine horse in front of his sons and driving the greatest herd of cattle in the county. Then I saw that he had a dead cigar in his mouth and a dead look on his face. The couple sat there on the wooden bench as gray and motionless as a plaster pop art sculpture.

I moved closer to them in the shadows. I wanted to run to Mrs. Cockshot and reinstate her to the power she had once held over me, but I couldn't bring myself to enter the strange, sad aura that surrounded them there under the tree.

I stared at the couple on the bench and tried to determine if they were as sad and lonely as they seemed, or if that was just the way people looked when they were living happily ever after. I decided that the two ideas were not incompatible, and satisfied with that conclusion, I moved out of the shadows under the trees.

I ran away from Mrs. Cockshot forever, without knowing that I was leaving a part of me with her that I would not need again. I ran back toward the harsh lights of the midway and the bounding music of the carousel. I ran to begin a new kind of tomorrow.

Think of Me

My parents were never prepared for a disruption in their lives. They took three children into the Florida backwoods to live, and they were shocked when we soon outgrew the meager provision offered to us by our rural schools.

My brother and sister needed richer programs than the high school in Dade City offered at that time. Though he was not Catholic or religious, my brother transferred to St. Leo, a private Catholic school in the hills of San Antonio, where the priests inspired him academically and where he could play his beloved football. My sister went to live with my mother's family in Sarasota to finish high school and study at the Ringling Art School.

Then we learned that my new teacher at the Sweetgum Slough school would be an inexperienced young girl with no training. I was delighted, but my father swore and declared that the school board members must be idiots. My mother sighed and shook her head and said that she couldn't believe it.

"The idea!" she said.

By then, I was ten years old and about to enter sixth grade. I had grown a bit during the summer holidays, but I still looked like a much younger child than I was. And I still cried like a baby when things didn't go as I thought they should. My parents had hoped that I could stay in the Sweetgum school near them for a few more years, but they decided that I would have to go to a school in Dade City.

I howled in protest when they told me that I would change schools. I screamed and said that I wouldn't go to the city school. I would not leave my country friends and the little one-roomed schoolhouse that I viewed as a sort of ongoing womb. I climbed a tree and refused to come down, even after dark. Only later, when it finally became clear that my parents were not going to rescue me from either the darkness of night or the school lying in wait for me in Dade City, did I creep into the house. I saw from the unfamiliar expressions on their faces that they would not change their position no matter how pitiful my sobs sounded or how many trees I climbed or how many times I declared that I would run away. My father even said that if I decided to leave I should borrow the charmed stick from Horus in case I came upon Autry along the way.

I went to bed hating them and feeling a mighty loss of power. But by daylight my spirit had repaired itself, and my mother told me that we were going to Tampa to see a picture show, eat dinner, and buy some new school clothes at Maas Brothers.

It was a long, happy day. While my father went to see his doctor, my mother and I shopped. I bought a wonderful dress with a separate bolero. Both pieces were blue checkered on one side and solid blue on the other, which meant that the dress could be worn reversed. It could be all blue or all checkered, or I could wear it solid blue with a checkered bolero or with a blue bolero and a checkered dress. I thought it was intriguing. More than that, it was the first dress I had bought from a store. My mother could sew, and she made wonderful dresses for my sister and me. But this ready-made dress filled me with a new pride.

We went to Kress's and ate a hot meal at the food counter. For fifty cents, we had roast beef, green beans, and hot mashed potatoes with gravy. For an additional ten cents, we ordered hot caramel sundaes. During the depression years, money was scarce. My father struggled to get his young orange trees up out of the ground, but that day he made sure we had enough money left for the picture show.

We went to the Tampa Theatre to see the latest African camera safari adventure of Martin and Osa Johnson. There was a double feature, too, so we spent grateful hours resting there in the elaborate, air-conditioned theatre where stars twinkled in the dark art deco sky, white misty clouds drifted overhead, and Eddie Ford popped up and played the organ between showings.

The first weeks in the new school were a shifting collage of nightmare images. Unlike the little Sweetgum school, where we were safely contained in one room all day, the new school had a chaotic thing in place called the rotation system. It meant that we changed classrooms and teachers with each subject while harsh bells rang and several hundred raucous children from other classrooms scrambled out of their seats and into the hallway. Everyone shouted and slammed lockers. They all knew each other, and they knew where to go and how to find the bathrooms.

I went to the wrong classroom several times. I sat through geography twice with two different groups of children, because I was afraid to ask where I should be. I aligned myself behind a girl with big hair so the teacher wouldn't notice me, and once I took refuge in the girls' bathroom where I sat on a toilet seat with my feet pulled up, hugging my knees and hardly breathing for fear someone would discover me there.

I became obsessed with my blue-checkered dress. I wore it reversed. I ducked in and out of the bathroom to change the bolero from blue-checkered to solid blue and to change the dress from solid to checkered. I was late for the next class because of my compulsion to reorganize the dress. I entered classrooms filled with hope that someone would finally notice my magic dress. But no one did.

A big boy said, "Here comes the pigmy." A girl with corkscrew curls like Shirley Temple's, laughed. Those tormented days twisted into each other like bands of hot mud. I slogged through them, struggling to find an air bubble, groping for a foothold.

One day, I noticed the other new girl who always sat by herself in the cafeteria and wandered around the playground looking morbid. I studied her as we both watched the other children cavort during the break and joke with the teachers on recess duty.

Finally I went to stand near the solemn girl. She was two heads taller than I was, and when she turned to look at me, I saw that her face was pale and freckled under kinky bright copper hair. She wore round glasses with gold frames. I thought they looked nice with her shining hair, and I told her so. She squinted and looked down at me, and when she spoke, her voice was a low snarl, like a sick old cat.

"Crawl back under your log!"

She turned and walked away. She didn't want to be near me. She wanted to be with the laughing, noisy girls who danced around the teachers. So did I.

Arithmetic class came just before lunch. Even after I learned how to get there, I dreaded it so much that I was unable to concentrate in my other classes. In Mrs. Cockshot's school, we all learned at the pace of the slowest pupils. As a result, I was behind the others in the new school. Long division was a mystery to me and fractions were nonexistent. I saw arithmetic not as a collection of human agreements, which might have made it more friendly, but as an entity unto itself—like rain or sky or some other nonnegotiable thing. My brain went limp when the teacher called on me to answer a question. Even when I knew the answer, I couldn't find my voice for fear I would be wrong.

I didn't know it then, but Mrs. McCann, the teacher, had only a superficial understanding of her subject, and she used it to glorify some students and to degrade and humiliate others. Arithmetic class taught us who was smart and who was dumb. And we were either smart or dumb from then on—an axiom established by Mrs. McCann who knew her facts.

English and reading were more manageable for me, but the material was dull. My father and mother read all kinds of books to me, which were usually whatever they were reading. That was a great blessing, even though it caused me to stare out of the window at school and daydream of Gatsby and Daisy. But the teacher was youthful and pleasant, and unlike so many teachers, she was polite to children. She must have sensed my unhappy condition, because she smiled one day and admired my blue dress when I wore it with the checkered bolero. She watched and listened with interest when I demonstrated the various personalities of the famous dress. She even said, "My goodness!" But such momentary release from the reign of terror all around me was not enough to get me through the day with my integrity intact.

American history class had one great advantage. High on the wall behind the teacher, there was a portrait of Martha Washington in a funny little bonnet. I found that if I looked at it long enough, I could see Mrs. Cockshot's broad, powdered face in the frilly bonnet, and for a while, I would be back in the Sweetgum schoolroom with Delano and Belle. Indulging in that sweet reverie didn't improve my listening skills in American history, but it provided an escape from the dreary barrage of misrepresentations issuing from the teacher's desk.

Mrs. Marlowe was an older woman with thinning gray hair and blotched, ruddy skin. Dates of all kinds fascinated her. I imagined that her dissected brain would look like a hornet's nest, from which she could release little date pellets on demand and send them out into the world to buzz around and intimidate children.

Along with American history, Mrs. Marlowe taught us a form of hysterical patriotism. By then, Adolf Hitler was making threatening moves in Europe. People in the United States were watching in numb disbelief as they faced the possibility of another war, and some of them reacted in peculiar ways. When a brazen, bright boy named Grady asked Mrs. Marlowe why she was so sure that democracy was the best form of government, she rose from her chair as though stricken to the deepest interior of her patriotic gut, and with a thin, rigid arm and a long arthritic index finger, she ordered Grady from the room and promised to set him straight later.

It was a dazzling scene. I was awash in a torrent of conflicting thoughts, rapids and eddies rushing and curling around my mind. I admired Grady. I wondered why it was a bad question. I thought it must be a bad question. I wondered if Grady were a bad boy. Most of all, I was glad that I was not Grady, and I told myself that I would never say anything in Mrs. Marlow's American history class again—especially when the subject was democracy.

Money was in meager supply everywhere, and art was not offered in that school. We were lucky to have music for the last period on Friday. I looked forward to music class all week. Not only did it mean that the week was over, but the buxom young teacher was not rude or neurotic, and I liked to sing. The songs we sang with her were different from the spirited tunes Mrs. Cockshot had taught us. In the new school, we sang soothing songs that were more suitable for a nursing home than for ten-year-old children. So they were just right for me.

After music, I boarded the rickety school bus, where I sat like a drugged, ancient person, not seeing the cypress swamps and orange groves as they jiggled by my window, the words of the last song still playing in my head. At last the bus stopped on the hardroad at the end of our lane. I opened the gate and followed a grassy rut to our house set back in the pines. I saw my father taking a coffee break on the porch. He was talking to Balder, who was smiling and wagging his tail. I sat down on the top step, and Balder collapsed on the floor close to me like an armload of firewood. I stroked his handsome black head.

"You look squashed," my father said. "Want a cup of coffee?"

"No. Where's Mama?" I asked.

"She went to San An," he said. "How was school?"

"Just like yesterday. And the day before. And the day before that. Every day something mean happens to me," I answered.

"It will get better. Nothing lasts forever. When they know you better, it will change. Just hang on. Tough it out. You can," he said.

"Well, at least they can't kill me," I told him. That idea had bolstered me daily. As I boarded the school bus each morning, I reminded myself that it was against the law to kill children in schools.

"That's right," he said. "And what doesn't kill you makes you stronger," he added, quoting Nietzsche.

"Why do people have to be sad and scared to get stronger? I was strong enough. I felt fine the way I was," I told him.

"Things change. That changed, and this will change. And what comes after this will change, too," he said. "Sooner or later."

I looked at him. "Maybe if I had curls like Shirley Temple it would change faster. Most of the girls have curls, and they're not sad or scared. Maybe I should get a permanent wave."

"What? Oh, for God's sake! Then who will go to the barber with me?" he said. My father and I had our hair cut together. I wore a Dutch bob, a simple short square cut with bangs. "You look perfect. Your hair fits your face just right. Why would you want to look like that fat-tailed, phony little midget?" My father stood up. He was wearing his work clothes over his six-foot-four-inch frame. "Do you want to look like this?"

He put his arms out at his sides, his hands turned upward, and began to tap dance in his size twelve brogans. He tossed his head as though it were full of ringlets, pouted his lips, twinkled his eyes, and looked more lunatic than lollipop. I had to laugh, in spite of my misery. Balder scrambled out of his sleep and barked at my father, who finished the performance and sat back down in his chair.

"It doesn't have anything to do with your hair," he said. "It's a matter of time. Just get through it. Stick it out. It will get better."

"But what will I do between now and then?" I asked. "I'm scared, and I feel dumb."

"Well, when you feel like that, think about something else. Think about something you like to do. Like eating ice cream or going to the beach. Or playing with a kitten."

"But that will only last a second," I said.

"Then you'll have to think of something that lasts longer. Like a good story. Or a long walk. Or love." He lifted his eyebrows the way he did when he had a good idea. "Think about love."

In those days, people didn't go around talking about love. No one said "I love you" when we left for school or when we came home or when we went to bed or got up. No one said it to console themselves or to sound spiritual or just for nothing. It would have been an odd thing to say. If our parents loved us, we knew it. If they didn't, saying that they did would not have worked. So when my father mentioned love, he had my attention.

He leaned forward in his chair, his face close to mine. There was a sadness in his blue eyes that I had never seen there.

"Think of someone you love. Or think of someone who loves you." His voice broke and recovered. "When you're in trouble, think of me," he said. And again, "Think of me."

Christmas 1937

your eyes
dulled blue
seeing yesterdays
and tomorrows
only you

could see
white stockings
white shoes
elevators sad
with silent people
sterile hallways
and sounds and smells
of dread

and then you said,
what will you do?
my mother
turned her head

away from you
she couldn't watch you die
or let you see her cry

Christ, what will you do?
you didn't know
how brave we were
you never knew
you never knew